A SHORT HISTORY
OF THE LABOUR PARTY

By F. Bealey and Henry Pelling

*

LABOUR AND POLITICS, 1900–1906

A SHORT HISTORY
OF THE
LABOUR PARTY

BY

HENRY PELLING
Fellow of The Queen's College, Oxford

LONDON
MACMILLAN & CO LTD
NEW YORK · ST MARTIN'S PRESS
1961

MACMILLAN AND COMPANY LIMITED
London Bombay Calcutta Madras Melbourne

THE MACMILLAN COMPANY OF CANADA LIMITED
Toronto

ST MARTIN'S PRESS INC
New York

PRINTED IN GREAT BRITAIN

CONTENTS

LIST OF ILLUSTRATIONS

The photograph of Arthur Henderson is by the *Daily Herald*: the other photographs are from the *Radio Times* Hulton Picture Library.

CHAPTER I

The New Party: Ideal and Reality
(To 1906)

(1)

AT the end of February 1960 the Labour Party could have celebrated (though it did not) its diamond jubilee. As an institution it was sixty years old, having been founded in 1900, although for the first six years of its life its title was different. From the inaugural conference until just after the general election of January 1906, its activities were conducted under the more modest title of the 'Labour Representation Committee'.

How did the Labour Representation Committee (or L.R.C. as we must call it) come into existence, and how did it succeed in transforming itself into a Labour Party? The long-term reasons were complex. It was partly because the enfranchisement of the manual workers in 1867 and in 1884 tended to increase the electoral importance of 'labour' and its leaders. But this factor by itself would not have been enough, as we know from our observation of American politics. Why was 'labour' a more or less homogeneous force in British politics, at least at the turn of the century? And why could it not adapt one or other of the existing parties to its purposes? The answer to the first of these additional questions takes us into the realm of the sociologist and economic historian; but it may be tentatively suggested that various social and economic changes were in the later nineteenth century leading in the direction of a greater solidarity of manual workers, partly by raising the standards of the unskilled workers to a level somewhat closer to that of the artisans, and partly by depressing, or at least threatening, the relative position of the artisans; and in some cases, by reason of the growth of industrial technology, by eliminating or very much reducing the differential of skill between 'general labour' and 'the trades'. As for the possibility of adapting one of the existing political parties to the purposes of 'labour', the answer must be made in terms of a study of existing political structure, and particularly that of the Liberal Party, to which the larger proportion of labour leaders belonged: it seems that the Liberal associations in the constituencies were too inflexible to adapt themselves to the rise of a new social class.

Early in the nineteenth century, there had been little concept of 'labour' as a single distinct class in the community. As Professor Asa Briggs has shown, it was more usual to speak of 'the labouring classes' or 'the middle classes' in the plural, thus recognising the variety to be found under both descriptions. During the 1870's and 1880's, however, the concept of a single 'working class', as also of a single 'middle class', began to develop. The Education Act of 1870 tended to separate the population more clearly into those who were educated at their parents' expense and those who went to the 'Board' schools or the church schools; nearly all the manual workers fell into the latter category. Furthermore, from the 1880's the unskilled workers were able to imitate the artisans in forming unions of their own, which were accepted into the company of the societies of the skilled men by being admitted to the Trades Union Congress. At the same time, the 'trades' themselves were being transformed by the mechanisation of industry and the growth of the scale of production: factory work replaced the work of the individual craftsman in more and more occupations as the 'industrial revolution' slowly spread through industries which had remained almost unchanged in their basic processes for centuries — shoemaking, for instance, or printing, which were both much affected in this period; and the close personal contact and collaboration between master and workman became a thing of the past. Thus it was that the unskilled labourer, concerned to achieve some minimum standards for himself and his family and to safeguard himself against unemployment, found allies in the ranks of the disgruntled artisans. Some of both groups took up with Socialism — a creed advocating a complete transformation of capitalist society, and often as in William Morris's writings hinting at a return to the age of the independent craftsman — but in the 1880's and 1890's it was in fact only a tiny minority of the so-called 'working class' which had as yet responded to 'the cause'. Like most new political faiths, Socialism started out as the enthusiasm of a few middle-class leaders; and the comparative prosperity of the employed workers in the late nineteenth century limited the success of the Socialists' appeal.

If its Socialist enthusiasm was not strong, why did not the newly enfranchised 'working class', with its growing homogeneity, not infiltrate and capture the bastions of an existing political party, and in particular, the Liberal Party? Certainly the Liberal Party seemed likely to be open to some such infiltration, for it was already a coalition of political forces whose relative strength varied from time to time, and it contained a radical wing which had made a strong appeal for working-class support. Unfortunately, however, in the 1870's and 1880's its structure had become rather rigid, and its leadership lacked both the power and the will to alter the situation. The local Liberal associations, largely in the hands of business and professional men and Nonconformist ministers, would rarely adopt working men as candidates, partly because they would have to take on the burden of paying the election expenses and upkeep of a poor man, and partly because their own special interests would suffer if the 'labour question' were thrust to the fore. The ageing Gladstone, obsessed with his 'mission' to 'pacify Ireland', would not take up the questions which seemed vital to young labour leaders, such as the state payment of M.P.s; and it was against his principles to venture into the vast field of social legislation if he could possibly avoid it.

As a result of all this, in 1893 an Independent Labour Party was formed at Bradford with the object of sending working men to Parliament, independent of both the Liberal and Conservative Parties. Its leaders admitted that they had been impressed by the success of the Irish Nationalists under Parnell in concentrating the attention of the major parties on the Irish question; they hoped to do the same thing for questions of social reform. The new body adopted a Socialist constitution, but, as can be seen from its name, it expected to win support from the workers whether they were Socialists or not. Several of its early leaders were men whose main objection to the Liberal Party was that it had failed to adopt them as Liberal candidates. This was the case with Keir Hardie, the Scottish miner who sat as an Independent Labour M.P. in the 1892 Parliament and who came to be regarded as the embodiment of the I.L.P. idea. The organisation also drew strength from the members of the new unions of the unskilled, who feared that without some sort of legislative assistance their industrial gains would be swept away in the next trade depression. After its foundation, the party also drew support from those who were disappointed with the Liberal Party after Gladstone's retirement. For when the 'Grand Old Man' at last retired in 1894, his successor, chosen by Queen Victoria, was Lord Rosebery, a young aristocrat with little popular appeal, whose most remarkable success was to win the Derby twice during his premiership (a remarkable feat, as his government lasted for only fifteen months), and who later emerged as a strong supporter of British imperial expansion in Africa and elsewhere.

Yet in 1899–1900, when the inauguration of the Labour Representation Committee was actually being undertaken, the I.L.P. and the other Socialist organisations (the Social-Democratic Federation and the Fabian Society) were pitiably weak, and as imperialism became the major issue of British politics they had been rapidly losing members. The country was in the grip of a jingoistic fervour which rose to a climax in the South African War; and the Socialists

4

suffered, not only because their primary concern was with domestic politics, but also because in most cases they actively opposed the war. To understand why it was that the Trade Union Congress agreed in the summer of 1899 to sponsor a meeting on labour representation, and also why the delegates who attended the resulting conference in February 1900 did manage to agree on the establishment of permanent machinery, we must turn to an examination of trade-union vicissitudes in the course of the 1890's.

(2)

In the last decade of the nineteenth century there were many reasons to make trade unionists and especially their officials feel insecure and anxious to obtain direct parliamentary representation. There had been a strong employers' reaction against the sudden expansion of unionism at the end of the 1880's, and this led them to search for every possible method of turning the tide. At the same time, the growth of industry, its national consolidation, and its new forms of organisation were all factors making for uncertainty in industrial relations. It was easy to believe, however, that the undermining of the legal position of the unionism as understood since the acts of the 1870's was due to a deliberate attempt to crush trade unionism.

Certainly the foundation in 1893 of a National Free Labour Association, to supply 'blacklegs' to take the place of workmen on strike, was a direct attack on unionism. But this body was not in fact very successful and its main influence was often to strengthen the resolve of strikers rather than to beat down their resistance. More important as a permanent threat was the growth of national federations of employers: the best example was the Federation of Engineering Employers, which in 1897–8 conducted the first national strike or lock-out, that of the engineering firms against the Amalgamated Society of Engineers. Worried by the success of German and American competition, the employers were inclined to think that the best

5

way to improve their competitive position was to reduce
costs by reducing wages, and they observed with envy
the comparative weakness of unionism in other countries,
particularly in the United States. In 1898 the further
important step was taken of forming an Employers' Parliamentary Council, which was designed to promote the
interests of employers generally at Westminster.

The legal rights of trade unions, up to the 1890's, had
apparently been defined by the Trade Union Acts of 1871
and 1876 and the Conspiracy and Protection of Property
Act, 1875. But a series of lawsuits in the 1890's changed
the situation, and because these cases were sometimes
finally decided by the House of Lords as the final arbiter,
labour leaders often jumped to the conclusion that these
decisions were political in character. It is certainly possible that political considerations influenced the judges, just
as in America the Supreme Court is said to 'follow the
election returns'. But the willingness of the Lords in their
judicial capacity to allow trade unions to be sued for the
tortious acts of their officials — something which the union
officials had thought to be impossible under earlier legislation — unquestionably owed a good deal to the general
development of company law, and particularly to the
appearance of the device known as the 'representative
action'. The law about union liability was not, however,
finally decided in the 1890's; and at the turn of the century union officials were primarily concerned about their
rights of picketing, now seriously restricted by a case known
as *Lyons* v. *Wilkins*, which had gone no further than the
Court of Appeal. If unionists could not picket, they were
virtually powerless to carry on a strike effectively. The
Employers' Parliamentary Council interested itself in this
decision, and issued a statement to its members pointing
out that picketing had now become 'almost harmless'.

It was in this situation that the 1899 Trade Union
Congress, meeting as usual in September, had to consider
a resolution from the Amalgamated Society of Railway
Servants to summon a special conference of trade unions,

co-operative societies, and Socialist bodies in order to make
plans for labour representation in Parliament. The proposal had come originally from the Doncaster branch of
the Railway Servants, where it had been put forward by
an I.L.P. member, Thomas R. Steels, who had served a
term on the union's national executive. As a Socialist, he
wanted to see the new organisation keep clear of the existing political parties, and his resolution was completely in
line with the policy of Keir Hardie and the other leaders of
the I.L.P. The support of the T.U.C. might not have been
forthcoming, however, if the resolution had been too out-
spoken on the question of political independence. As it
was, it was hotly debated, and opposed by the miners, who
could already by virtue of the concentration of membership
in particular areas elect M.P.s without help from other
unions, forcing the Liberal Party to accept their candidates.
(These were the so-called 'Lib-Labs'.) Nevertheless, the
resolution was carried, by 546,000 votes against 434,000.
About a third of the delegates must have abstained from
voting, and to judge by those who spoke in the debate, the
main supporters were the leaders of the new unskilled
unions, who evidently hoped that parliamentary representation would be a valuable safeguard of the future existence of their organisations.

After the Congress was over, there was some conflict
between the conservative T.U.C. Parliamentary Committee
— which represented the T.U.C. in between meetings of
Congress — and the Socialist leaders as to who should make
the arrangements for the conference on labour representation, and how the agenda should be drawn up. But the
conference finally met on 27th and 28th February 1900,
in the Memorial Hall, near Ludgate Circus, and this
meeting has always been looked upon as 'the foundation
of the Labour Party'. Yet at the time it was not looked
upon as having accomplished this. All that the delegates
did was to establish a committee to promote and co-ordinate
plans for labour representation: something comparable
with the Labour Representation League of 1869, or the

Labour Electoral Committee of 1886. The financial arrangements made to support the committee were very limited and simple: organisations affiliated to it were to pay no more than 10s. per thousand members, and on such a basis the committee could neither appoint any paid official nor finance any candidatures of its own. No political programme was agreed upon and it was not even decided whether the new body was to work in collaboration with one or other of the existing political parties, as its predecessors had done, or to establish an independent party of its own.

As nobody seemed to want the job, the I.L.P. had no difficulty in securing the secretaryship for their nominee, Ramsay MacDonald, then a young journalist. It was also fortunate that Frederick Rogers, the first chairman of the executive, though not a Socialist, was at least keen to see the new body established on a firm footing. Rogers drastically altered Keir Hardie's draft for the organisation's first circular, as he put it, 'with an eye to the oldfashioned trade unionist, who if he cannot push us forward may be a very dead weight indeed to hold us back'.[1] Even the moderation of Rogers, however, could make no impact on the co-operative leaders, and after attending the national co-operative conference in 1900 he declared that he was 'hardly prepared for the solid unbending Toryism of the older men, and the meek acquiescence or flippant contempt of the younger ones, in relation to social affairs'.[2] Under these circumstances, the committee had to abandon hope of winning the support of the co-operative societies.

There were, of course, obvious technical reasons why even the most 'advanced' unions might be slow to join. Their constitutions imposed cumbersome delays in making decisions, and although some secretaries or executive councils were empowered to take action of this character, it was more commonly thought necessary or desirable to consult the membership by referendum or to leave the matter to an annual or biennial conference. Where a referendum was undertaken, the apathy of the membership militated against

KEIR HARDIE (1856–1915)

a clear-cut decision, for a majority in a very small poll was not always regarded as binding. George Barnes, the secretary of the Amalgamated Society of Engineers, and himself a member of the I.L.P., was forced to write to the L.R.C. to say that 'the members of the Society have evinced so little interest in the question of Parliamentary representation that we cannot see how we can take part'.[3]

Generally speaking, the unions which joined in the first year were the new unions of the unskilled, partly because their constitutions tended to be more centralised, and partly because their officers were more inclined to believe in political action — several of them in fact being Socialists. In addition, however, there was the Amalgamated Society of Railway Servants, which had initiated the conference by its T.U.C. resolution and which stood to gain very much by representation in Parliament, where so much railway legislation was discussed and enacted. If we add the two main printers' unions and the Boot and Shoe Workers — all of whom were suffering from rapid technological change and who seem to have been in a particularly radical mood — we have accounted for about two-thirds of the union membership of the Labour Representation Committee at the end of its first year.

In addition, of course, there were the Socialist societies: the I.L.P., the Social-Democratic Federation or S.D.F. (a Marxist group), and the Fabians. These bodies had by decision of the inaugural conference secured representation on the committee out of all proportion to their membership and financial contribution. The Fabians had one seat and the other bodies two seats each: thus they had five seats out of a total of twelve on the committee, and in addition the secretary of the committee, the only full-time (albeit unpaid) officer of the organisation, was a nominee of the I.L.P. Yet the Socialist societies in the first year provided only about 6 per cent of the funds. The charges of Socialist dictation and control of the new organisation would certainly have had a great deal of substance, if it had not been that the three societies were at odds with one another. The

S.D.F., dissatisfied at the refusal of the inaugural conference and of the conference a year later to accept the 'class war' concept, retired from membership and their two seats on the committee disappeared; and Edward Pease, the Fabian representative, opposed the I.L.P. attempt to make the L.R.C. into a new political party and found himself on the 'unionist' as against the 'Socialist' side on nearly all issues of disagreement. Much continued to depend, therefore, upon the enthusiasm of the non-Socialist union leaders for this new form of political action.

(3)

The first general election fought by the L.R.C. took place only six months after its inauguration. When the Unionist government dissolved in the summer, the crisis of the South African War had just been surmounted, and it could expect to benefit from the wave of patriotic enthusiasm then affecting all classes — and not least the working class. Fifteen candidates sponsored by individual unions or by Socialist societies were endorsed by the L.R.C., although the L.R.C. could not do more for them than provide a small supply of leaflets and its best wishes. The total L.R.C. expenditure on the general election amounted to only £33. Under these circumstances, it was more the result of its good fortune than of its efforts that two of its candidates were returned to Parliament. At Derby, Richard Bell, the secretary of the Railway Servants, was elected in the company of a Liberal for a two-member seat; and at Merthyr, Keir Hardie had the same experience. Hardie, it may be said, owed his success entirely to the fortunate coincidence that the Welsh miners opposed the South African War, while one of the two Liberals seeking re-election at Merthyr did not.

With only two M.P.s, however, the L.R.C. could not make much impression in Parliament, especially as Bell and Hardie were not very compatible. Hardie was a Socialist who favoured an independent stand on many questions;

Bell was virtually nothing but a Liberal except on questions of direct importance to his union, the Railway Servants. The general election also returned several 'Lib-Labs' — only eight, as against twelve at the dissolution, but enough to prevent the two L.R.C. men from being regarded as representative of Labour in general. Consequently, although the L.R.C. could claim the election results as creditable, it could not hope that they would do much to convince unaffiliated unions of the importance of joining their ranks.

What really strengthened the willingness of trade-union officers to recommend affiliation to the L.R.C. was the Taff Vale judgment by the House of Lords in July 1901. This decision emerged from a strike on the Taff Vale railway in 1900, during which the general manager of the railway company, following the advice of the Employers' Parliamentary Council, brought actions for damages against the Secretary of the Railway Servants for picketing the Cardiff stations. The judgment reaffirmed *Lyons* v. *Wilkins* on picketing and also declared that the union's funds were liable for the tortious acts of its officials. The Taff Vale Railway Company could go ahead and secure damages from the Railway Servants, and in fact a total of £23,000 had to be paid — a figure which included the company's costs, but not the union's.

As was to be expected, the impact of such a complicated legal decision caused much confusion, but most union leaders soon began to realise that they had suffered a serious setback in their ceaseless struggle against the employers. Although they continued to press the existing parties in the House of Commons to pass legislation restoring the *status quo ante* Taff Vale, and although they found the Liberal Party (which was of course in opposition) to be generally favourable, they also moved in increasing numbers to the support of the Labour Representation Committee, which promised to help them to elect their own members as M.P.s. Consequently the L.R.C. membership rose from 376,000 early in 1901 to 469,000 a year later and 861,000 in 1903.

The largest reinforcements came from the adhesion of the Textile Workers — a group of unions with altogether more than a hundred thousand members. This occurred largely as the result of a by-election in the weaving constituency of Clitheroe, where the secretary of the Cotton Weavers, David Shackleton, was adopted by the L.R.C. Philip Snowden, who was being considered as an I.L.P. candidate, won much credit by withdrawing in Shackleton's favour. The union's strength in the constituency was so great that although it had previously been a Liberal seat, neither the Liberals nor the Conservatives felt able to challenge Shackleton's return, albeit he described himself simply as a Labour candidate. Shackleton's unopposed success was followed by a ballot of the Textile Workers to decide whether they favoured parliamentary representation, and on the affirmative result of the ballot the Textile Workers early in 1903 joined the L.R.C. in a body. The Engineers had also joined in the course of 1902, after the prolonged constitutional wrestling that always seemed to be necessary for major decisions in this union. As a result, the only large unions not yet in the L.R.C. were those of the miners, whose success in electing their own members as 'Lib-Labs' continued to inhibit their enthusiasm for joining in with the other unions or abandoning the Liberal Party.

With all this additional support, the L.R.C. at its third conference at Newcastle in February 1903 was able to consolidate itself and tighten its constitution. The subscription rate was increased and furthermore a compulsory parliamentary fund was established for the payment of M.P.s. The result was that the payment made by the affiliated unions and Socialist societies went up from 10s. per thousand members to almost £5. The payment of M.P.s obviously provided an effective way of asserting discipline over Members of Parliament and candidates; and the conference could expect to be obeyed when it also decided that henceforth its candidates must 'strictly abstain from identifying themselves with or promoting the interests of any section of the Liberal or Conservative parties'.

These changes added a great deal both to the strength and to the independence of the L.R.C., making it more of a new 'party' than ever before. Yet at the same time they increased the eagerness of the Liberal Chief Whip, Herbert Gladstone, to come to some terms with the L.R.C. The expectation of an early general election, owing to disagreements in the Unionist Cabinet about Tariff Reform, increased the urgency of the matter. Accordingly, Gladstone and Ramsay MacDonald secretly negotiated an agreement to enable the L.R.C. to put up most of its candidates without the need to face Liberal opposition.

The Unionist Government did not fall in 1903, and so the danger of an immediate election was averted. Even so, the agreement between MacDonald and Gladstone was confirmed and, although secret, was remarkably effective in avoiding clashes between L.R.C. and Liberal candidates — at least in England, but not in Scotland where the writ of the National Liberal Federation did not run. This was in spite of the enthusiasm of local organisations on both sides — Liberal associations and local L.R.C.s — to put up candidates and make a fight against all comers. On the side of the L.R.C., probably only Keir Hardie was fully in the know about the agreement, and local branches of the I.L.P. were particularly embarrassing in their demands for contests. They could, however, largely be held in check by lack of financial backing from the centre and by the argument that the I.L.P. could not claim more than a proportion of the total L.R.C. candidatures.

It was fortunate, moreover, that the rapprochement of Liberal and Socialist opinion, which had begun when both the Radicals and the I.L.P. opposed the South African War, was confirmed by the new issues raised by the Unionists during their remaining term of office. Both Liberals and L.R.C. supporters (the Fabians alone excepted) could unite in opposition to the 1902 Education Act, which seemed to damage the interests of the Nonconformists; both too could denounce the Chamberlain plan for Tariff Reform, which from 1903 onwards rapidly became the leading political

13

controversy of the time. Both also found an emotive if somewhat ephemeral slogan in 'Chinese labour', for the introduction of Chinese indentured labour in South Africa was alarming both on humanitarian grounds and on the grounds of the competition that it would afford with British emigrant labour.

Meanwhile the L.R.C. was able to establish a record of by-election successes, which more and more convinced the Liberals of the value of co-operation. Following the un-opposed success at Clitheroe, in March 1903 Will Crooks, a popular Cockney working man, with Liberal support won a straight fight against a Unionist candidate at Woolwich : this victory strengthened MacDonald's hand in his negotia-tions with Herbert Gladstone. In May of the same year, John Hodge, the secretary of the Steel Smelters, polled un-expectedly well, although unsuccessfully, in the Tory strong-hold of Preston; and in July Arthur Henderson of the Ironfounders won a seat from the Liberals in a three-cor-nered contest at Barnard Castle. The return of Crooks and Henderson as well as Shackleton brought the L.R.C. mem-bership of the Commons up to a theoretical total of five, but Bell was showing reluctance to abide by the require-ments of independence as stated at the L.R.C. conference of 1903, and in 1904 he was officially regarded as having lapsed from the group. As none of the recently elected trio was a Socialist or a keen independent, MacDonald and Hardie had a good deal of difficulty in keeping them on the narrow line of political separation from the Liberals : and indeed their task was all the harder in view of their own secret commitment to co-operation with the Liberals by the MacDonald-Gladstone electoral agreement.

(4)

When the election finally took place in January 1906, it was clear that MacDonald's plans for its conduct on the Labour side had worked out perfectly. The L.R.C. had in all fifty candidates, as it had intended; forty of them were sponsored by individual trade unions, by trades councils or

by local L.R.C.s, and a further ten were sponsored by the
I.L.P. Only eighteen of the fifty were opposed by Liberal
candidates, and of these eighteen, some faced only unofficial candidates on the Liberal side. In ten double-member
constituencies, one Liberal and one L.R.C. candidate fought
side by side against Conservative opposition. The co-operation between Liberals and the L.R.C. was most complete
in Lancashire, which had lately been a strong Conservative
area and which was not expected to show much change unless some such electoral alliance was effected. In Wales and
Yorkshire, on the other hand, where Liberalism remained
fairly strong, its leaders had felt less need for concessions to
Labour; in Scotland they made none at all.

If the main issue of the general election had been social
reform, it might have been possible to detect some conflict
between Liberal and L.R.C. candidates, and some difference between the electoral support that they obtained, in
spite of the electoral agreement. In fact, however, the
issues of the election were simply those which differentiated
most of the Liberals from the Conservatives: Tariff Reform,
'Chinese Labour', Education, and (a rather poor fourth)
Home Rule for Ireland. The tide ran strongly in the
direction of Liberalism, especially in Lancashire, where
Tariff Reform seemed to threaten the established foreign
markets of the cotton trade. The result was that the Liberals
secured 377 seats, giving them a majority of 84 over all
other parties combined. In the Liberal wake, the L.R.C.
secured 29 seats, no less than 12 of them being in Lancashire.

Of the twenty-nine L.R.C. men in the new Parliament,
seven, including Hardie, MacDonald, and Snowden, were
sponsored by the I.L.P. The remainder, although sponsored by trade unions or local labour bodies, also contained
a good many members of the I.L.P., and one (Will Thorne,
the secretary of the Gasworkers Union) was a member of
the S.D.F. It was equally significant, however, that of the
successful twenty-nine, only five were elected against Liberal
opposition, and at least two of these five had faced only
unofficial Liberal opposition. Two of the other three were

the L.R.C.'s sole representatives from Scotland. Altogether ten members — more than a third of the party — were elected in two-member constituencies, where the other member was a Liberal. All of the twenty-nine new M.P.s were of working-class origin, and this had in fact been true of all the fifty candidates, except for one, Stanton Coit, who was an American. Several of them were the secretaries of important unions — the Gasworkers, the Steel Smelters, the Shipwrights, and the Engineers — while others had had long careers as officials of unions; many of them were under a vague Socialist influence, but only one or two were Marxists. Most of them claimed to be devoutly religious — nearly all being some sort of Methodist, or Congregationalist.

The success of the L.R.C. created a sensation at the time, and Balfour, the defeated Unionist leader, went so far as to suggest that the new Liberal Prime Minister, Campbell-Bannerman, was a 'mere cork' on the Socialist tide. In reality, as even a few Socialists including Bernard Shaw pointed out at the time, it was largely the other way about: the L.R.C. was a cork on the Liberal tide, and if any 'ism' was triumphant in 1906 it was Gladstonianism.

NOTES

1. Rogers to MacDonald, 13 Mar. 1900, Labour Party Letter Files, Transport House.
2. Rogers to MacDonald, 30 May 1900, *ibid.*
3. Barnes to MacDonald, 7 Nov. 1900, *ibid.*

FURTHER READING

A fuller narrative and discussion of the issues raised in this chapter will be found in Henry Pelling, *Origins of the Labour Party, 1880–1900* (1954), and in Frank Bealey and Henry Pelling, *Labour and Politics, 1900–6* (1958). A more succinct account, though weak on the industrial side, is Philip P. Poirier, *Advent of the Labour Party* (1958). Among recent literature, the reader may also refer to Asa Briggs (ed.), *Essays in Labour History* (1960), which contains useful essays by Asa Briggs and by John Saville on 'The Language of "Class"' and 'Trade Unions and Free Labour' respectively.

The New Party: Ideal and Reality (To 1906)

G. D. H. Cole's *British Working Class Politics, 1832–1914* (1941), provides an outline of the electoral activity of labour. Some of the atmosphere of the period is effectively recreated in Joseph Clayton, *Rise and Decline of Socialism, 1884–1924* (1926), an undeservedly neglected book.

CHAPTER II

A Pressure-group under Pressure
(*1906–14*)

(1)

As soon as the 1906 Parliament assembled, the L.R.C.
assumed the name of 'Labour Party' and its twenty-nine
M.P.s elected officers and whips. The life of the party in
the following eight years, 1906–14, although undergoing
many vicissitudes, yet has a certain unity for analytical
purposes. The great tide of Liberal feeling, which had
brought the Labour Party to Parliament, ebbed considerably, as was shown by the two elections in 1910; and the
Labour Party, only too much like a cork, ebbed with it, and
lost a few seats in the 1910 elections. The apparent increase
in the number of Labour M.P.s — from twenty-nine in
1906 to forty after the first 1910 election and forty-two
after the second 1910 election — is entirely accounted for
by the accession of most of the miners' M.P.s, formerly
'Lib-Labs', after the Miners Federation decided to join the
Labour Party in 1909. Furthermore, after the second 1910
election the Labour Party strength was reduced by the loss
of by-elections, and at the outbreak of war numbered only
thirty-seven, of whom twelve were miners' representatives.
It will be seen, then, that the record of the parliamentary
party in these eight years was not one of numerical advance
in any real sense.

It would have been to the advantage of the Labour
Party to dissociate itself from the Liberals, once it had a
fairly strong representation in Parliament, and to devise its
policies and propaganda on a basis of complete independence. The difficulties which prevented it from doing this,

however, were numerous. First of all, there was the character of the parliamentary situation, which obliged the party to vote either for or against proposals of the Liberal government. After all, there are only two voting lobbies in the House, and abstention is not an impressive way of representing one's constituency. The fact that from 1908 onwards the Liberals, under pressure from Lloyd George, did take a strong initiative on social reform obliged the Labour Party either to support the Liberal policy or risk criticism as opponents of practicable reform. After the first 1910 election, moreover, the Labour Party lost what freedom of action it had retained in the preceding four years owing to the government's lack of a clear majority. The support of the Labour Party and the Irish was essential if the government was to stay in office; and owing to its special financial difficulties at the time, the Labour Party did not dare to risk a fresh dissolution — at least, not after the second 1910 election, which it survived only with considerable difficulty.

There was also the special problem created by the success of the MacDonald-Gladstone electoral pact. As we have seen, many of the Labour M.P.s owed their election to Liberal support, and this was particularly obvious in the two-member constituencies, where several of them had been returned in harness with a Liberal. When by-elections occurred, as they sometimes did, owing to the decease or promotion of the Liberal M.P. in one of these two-member constituencies, the parliamentary party and MacDonald himself (who represented the two-member constituency of Leicester) were extremely reluctant to contest the vacancy, much to the irritation of the local branches of the I.L.P.

At the same time, there was the fact that the Labour Party was largely deficient in parliamentary and administrative talent, and it was incapable of producing satisfactory alternative policies of reform. The Labour M.P.s, as has already been pointed out, were all of working-class origin, and though some of them were quite able men, they lacked professional training and administrative experience. They had as yet no middle-class Fabians in their ranks, and in any case they distrusted the Fabian leaders, especially the Webbs and Bernard Shaw, because of their readiness to 'permeate' the older political parties with their ideas. In particular, Sidney Webb had had a part in shaping the Education Act of 1902, of which most of the Labour Party disapproved.

Of equal importance was the absence of cohesion in the party itself. This arose in part from the democratic traditions of the labour movement, which were by no means adjusted to the exigencies of parliamentary life. The Labour Party was in any case, as we have seen, a federation of independent organisations, and it was natural that the differences existing among the bodies sponsoring the M.P.s, and particularly those between the Socialist societies and the trade unions, should appear on the parliamentary scene. The difficulties were exemplified by almost the first act of the parliamentary party — the election of a chairman (he was not known, as in the case of the other parties, as a leader). There were two candidates: Hardie of the I.L.P., who was the Socialist candidate, and Shackleton of the Cotton Weavers, who was a non-Socialist trade union leader. On the first vote, which was an open one, the two men obtained equal support, Ramsay MacDonald as secretary of the extra-parliamentary party abstaining. Then, a ballot was held: MacDonald again abstained and the result was the same. Finally, a second ballot took place with MacDonald participating and Hardie was elected. The result of this division was that Hardie had to undertake not to make his chairmanship a permanent one, but to encourage a rotation of the office. Consequently he was succeeded in 1908 by Henderson who, as the Socialists put it, was one of the 'old gang' of trade-union leaders; and in 1910 Henderson was succeeded by George Barnes, the secretary of the Engineers. Barnes fell ill in 1911 and his place was then taken by MacDonald, whose parliamentary ability fully matched his administrative talents.

With the chairmanship changing hands so frequently,

and with major differences in any case existing in the political standpoint of the members of the party, it was inevitable that discipline was weak. Hardie himself proved to be an indifferent parliamentarian, rather inclined to play the lone wolf, and by no means ready to adapt himself to collective decisions. When at the 1907 Labour Party conference a resolution was passed opposing any women's suffrage legislation on a property franchise, Hardie at once said that he would resign from the parliamentary party rather than accept this as his policy. The parliamentary party therefore hastily passed a resolution allowing him to vote on this issue contrary to party policy.[1] In later years, this formed a valuable precedent for others who wished to express their own disagreements with the collective will: it was, in fact, the origin of the well-known 'conscience clause' which was embodied in the party's Standing Orders.

Hardie as chairman constantly left it to Henderson, the party whip, to negotiate 'behind the Speaker's chair' about the conduct of business; and in 1907 for a large part of the session he was away ill. When in 1908 Henderson became chairman, therefore, he was not without experience. But Hardie regarded him with grave suspicion as being little more than a Liberal. Hardie wrote a revealing letter to his I.L.P. colleague Bruce Glasier at the end of Henderson's first year of office:

I suppose we are in for another year of Henderson's chairmanship, which means that reaction and timidity will be in the ascendancy with disastrous effects to our side of the movement in the country. I grow weary of apologising for a state of things for which I am not responsible and with which I have scant sympathy. Then when the miners come in the Annual Conferences will be controlled by Coal and Cotton, and . . . that means more reaction. There are times when I confess to feeling sore at seeing the fruits of our years of toil being garnered by men who were never of us, and who even now would trick us out . . .[2]

This sort of mutual suspicion and disagreement resulted

in open conflicts on many issues, and after 1910 a distinct 'cave' of Socialist rebels, consisting of Hardie, Snowden, and Lansbury, made its appearance. MacDonald did not join them, and when he became chairman of the party he ran into just as much difficulty as Henderson had encountered with the Socialist rebels. As W. J. Braithwaite, the Treasury official helping to prepare the Insurance Act, said of the officials of the Labour Party in 1911 : 'They don't speak for their men, don't know what their men want, and can't bind their men to obey — rather difficult people to deal with'.[3]

(2)

If the Socialists inside the parliamentary party were restive and embittered with their trade-unionist colleagues, it goes without saying that the extra-parliamentary Socialists were even more restive and bitter. The rank and file of the I.L.P. resented the limitations on their activity that were imposed by their leaders' association with the Labour Party, and through the Labour Party, with the Liberals. The Trade Disputes Act (restoring the *status quo ante* Taff Vale) and the very limited Provision of School Meals Act — the two Labour successes of 1906 — cut very little ice with the Socialists. Their frustration found a striking expression as early as 1907, when a young I.L.P.er called Victor Grayson was put up as a candidate at a by-election in the Colne Valley. Grayson went about his adoption incorrectly and failed to get endorsement from the local union leaders. He consequently had to fight without the official support of the Labour Party. But he made a virtue of this necessity, and proclaiming himself a 'clean Socialist' he managed to win a former Liberal seat in a three-cornered contest. The result was startling to all the political parties, and embarrassing to the Labour Party. It may well be that it was this apparent 'boom' in Socialism which convinced Lloyd George of the need to press for social reform inside the Cabinet.

Grayson, at Westminster, was regarded as a pariah by

the Labour M.P.s. This was to a large extent his own fault, for he was anxious to make a sensation at Westminster rather than to seek allies with whom he might co-operate for constructive purposes. Keir Hardie, who had practised somewhat similar tactics in the 1890's, resented their continuation in a period when a Labour Party already existed. His resentment, however, would have been more justifiable if the Labour Party had in fact been winning attention for a constructive programme : yet as Hardie himself admitted this was not the case — indeed, he declared in 1910 that the Labour Party had 'almost ceased to count'.⁴

Part of the trouble, of course, lay in the fact that the Liberal Party under pressure from Lloyd George was taking the initiative from 1908 onwards. We still do not know how far Lloyd George as Chancellor of the Exchequer deliberately provoked the rejection of his budget by the House of Lords ; but he must have realised at an early stage that such a development was of much value to the Liberals, for it gave them a constitutional issue on which to go to the country — an issue that would unite their variegated supporters, who were still inclined to disagree about social reform, and at the same time an issue on which the Labour Party had nothing distinctive to propose. In fact, the reforms proposed in the 1909 budget — a tax on land values and a small supertax being the main novelties — were not particularly startling, but rather irritating ; and the Unionist majority in the Lords undoubtedly committed a serious tactical error in rejecting the budget, thereby putting themselves on dangerous constitutional ground.

With an election pending in 1909, the Labour Party was suddenly struck an unexpected blow in the law-courts. This was the Osborne Judgment, which declared its system of fund-raising from the trade unions to be illegal. Osborne was a member of the Amalgamated Society of Railway Servants who objected to paying a compulsory levy for the upkeep of the Labour M.P.s. He sought an injunction against the union, and this was upheld by the courts and on appeal by the House of Lords. The view taken by the

Lords was that, since political action was not mentioned among the legitimate objects of unions in the Trade Union Act of 1876, it was therefore illegal. The Lords also commented unfavourably upon the system whereby Labour M.P.s were obliged to give a pledge to abide by the party's instructions in their behaviour in the House of Commons.

This decision crippled the party financially, and various attempts made by the unions to continue their support for the Labour Party on a voluntary basis collapsed in the face of the apathy of their members. The party with the support of the T.U.C. determined to secure legislation to reverse the decision. In the meantime, it had to fight the two general elections of 1910, and in both its dependence upon the Liberals was very obvious. In the January election, not a single member was returned against official Liberal opposition; the same was true of the December election except for two mining seats.

In the earlier of these general elections Grayson was defeated. But he had already become of more significance outside Parliament than in it, for he was running a vigorous campaign to free the Socialist movement of the encumbrance of the 'Labour alliance', as he saw it. This campaign won support, not only from the dogmatically Marxist S.D.F. (as was to be expected), but also from a large proportion of the rank and file of the I.L.P. Ever since 1907 I.L.P. conferences had become a real test of strength for Keir Hardie and Ramsay MacDonald, and in 1909, after an unfavourable vote, Hardie, MacDonald, Snowden, and Bruce Glasier, the 'big four' of the I.L.P., all resigned from the Council of the organisation, although their policy was in the end endorsed.

In 1910 the campaign inside the I.L.P. went a stage further when four of the new members of the Council published a pamphlet entitled *Let Us Reform the Labour Party*. Known as the 'Green Manifesto' because of the colour of its cover, it fiercely denounced the leadership for abandoning the original position of the I.L.P., which, it said, was

RAMSAY MACDONALD (1866–1937)

that 'Labour must fight for Socialism and its own hand
against BOTH the Capitalist parties IMPARTIALLY'.[5] The
contest inside the I.L.P. became more embittered, but the
rebels failed to win control of the party, perhaps because
Grayson was not a good leader — he had taken heavily to
drink, and was very unreliable about attending meetings.

In 1911 the opponents of the 'Labour alliance', both
inside and outside the I.L.P., decided to found a new
united Socialist organisation. This took the name of
British Socialist Party (B.S.P.). The largest element in its
composition was the S.D.F., whose veteran leader, H. M.
Hyndman, became chairman of the new body. But it also
included many individual rebels and even whole branches
from the I.L.P., as well as other Socialists such as those
belonging to the Clarion Fellowship, which was sponsored
by Robert Blatchford's *Clarion* newspaper. At the end of
its first year of activity the B.S.P. claimed a membership
of some 15,000 — half the size of the I.L.P. at its peak.
Thereafter, the B.S.P. membership dwindled until at the
outbreak of war in 1914 it seemed to contain few more
than had been in the old S.D.F. By this time, furthermore,
it was seeking reaffiliation to the Labour Party.

The assault of the discontented Socialists upon the
alliance of the I.L.P. with the trade unionists was thus but
narrowly defeated in 1909–11, but for various reasons —
mainly the emergence of new issues — it weakened thereafter. In the course of 1911 a new challenge to the Labour
Party appeared among its own affiliated organisations. This
was a challenge inside the unions, and it arose from the
Syndicalist movement, which sought to dispense with politics,
or at least parliamentary politics, altogether. The object of
Syndicalism was to win control of the economy by industrial action, and as a first step it sought to turn the unions
into agents of its purpose, making them industrial unions
instead of craft unions, and effecting amalgamations of
small societies in the same or kindred industries. The most
prominent Syndicalist leader was Tom Mann, who had
come to public notice for his part in the 1889 dock strike,

but who since then for ten years or so had been working in New Zealand and Australia. Mann now reinforced his renown by successfully conducting a large-scale transport strike on Merseyside. The Syndicalist movement absorbed the energies of a good many of the more militant Socialists, and it consequently had a weakening effect on the B.S.P., but it did not make very much permanent impression upon the officialdom of the unions. Its greatest success was perhaps in the field of amalgamation, and in particular it led to the merging of the Railway Servants and two other railwaymen's unions into the National Union of Railwaymen. But its limited success even among railwaymen is shown by the continued existence of two other unions in the industry, the Locomotive Engineers and Firemen and the Railway Clerks. Nevertheless, a younger generation of trade unionists was much influenced by Syndicalism, perhaps especially the miners, who in these years as the price of coal went down, and with it, their wages, grew more and more impatient with their generally conservative leaders.

A further result of Syndicalism was that an interesting daily labour newspaper called the *Herald* came into existence. It was largely in the hands of George Lansbury, who was a left-wing Socialist owing a nominal allegiance to the I.L.P. Its contributors were all rebels of one sort or another, but not necessarily Syndicalists or even Socialists. They included many able men, for instance, G. K. Chesterton, Hilaire Belloc, the cartoonist Will Dyson, and the young Oxford don G. D. H. Cole, who evolved the idea of Guild Socialism as a sort of compromise between parliamentary action and the popular desire for workers' control of industry. The *Herald*, though perpetually in danger of financial collapse, was much more interesting than the official Labour newspaper, the *Daily Citizen*, which, sponsored by the Labour Party and the T.U.C., came into existence in 1912. It was significant that when war broke out in 1914 the *Daily Citizen* expired immediately, while the *Herald* managed to struggle on and to survive for a more important role in the post-war world.

(3)

As has been said, the most difficult time for the Labour Party was after the 1910 elections, when it had to sustain the Liberal Party in power at all costs, and at the same time seek from it the concession of legislation to reverse the Osborne Judgment. But the Liberals had their own programme of legislation, and all that the Labour Party could obtain in 1911 was the introduction of state payment of M.P.s, in return for which MacDonald gave Lloyd George a guarantee that the party would support his Insurance Bill.[6] The state payment of members was of advantage to the Labour Party in easing the financial problem facing its M.P.s, but it obviously weakened the discipline of the parliamentary party still further, particularly as it was felt desirable to abandon the practice introduced in 1903 of requiring the M.P.s or candidates to sign a pledge to observe the party's constitution and Standing Orders.

MacDonald himself, so far as one can tell, sincerely believed in the principles of Lloyd George's Insurance Act, and not least in the contributory principle, which many Socialists felt to be contrary to their faith. As he said in his Second Reading speech, 'I am in favour of insurance and not of free gift'.[7] On the other hand, Snowden and the Webbs, together with Lansbury who had served with Mrs. Webb on the Poor Law Commission, were united in opposition to this view. Their aim was a National Health Service undertaking preventive measures for the benefit of the whole community. The difficulty with this distinctly more Socialist view was the cost, which would be difficult to control, unlike the actuarially sound insurance scheme that Lloyd George introduced. Lloyd George's scheme, however, proved preferable to the trade unionists, once they understood that the unions would be approved societies for the purpose of the Act. The upshot was that most of the Labour Party supported the government in the lobbies on this question, and there was only a small minority of irreconcilable Socialists who joined the irreconcilable Tories in opposition to it.

In 1913 the unhappy position of Labour Party finances was cleared up by the passing of the Trade Union Act. Under the Act, trade unions were permitted to raise contributions from their members for political purposes, provided that they kept their political fund separate from their funds for industrial and general purposes. Union members were to be allowed to contract out of paying the contributions for political purposes if they desired to do so, simply by making a written statement of their intention. Opponents of the Labour Party in the Commons did not like this arrangement, as they felt that union members would be subject to intimidation to prevent them from contracting out. They suggested instead that union members should be regarded as non-contributors to the political fund unless they actually contracted in. But the latter view naturally did not commend itself to the Labour leaders in view of their recent experience with voluntary funds, and the bill went through in the form that they were prepared to accept.

By this time the government was finding, amidst all its other distractions, including the great struggle over Irish Home Rule, that an ever greater proportion of the budget had to be devoted to armaments, particularly for a naval building programme to keep well ahead of the German effort. The majority of Labour M.P.s, together with a substantial minority of Liberals, favoured resistance to this tendency. For ideological reasons, they were quite as suspicious of Russia as of Germany, and they held that the best thing for Britain to do was to keep out of continental quarrels by a policy of isolation. Many of them regarded military expenditure as an unwelcome diversion of funds which might otherwise be spent on social reform.

The Socialists were also inclined to oppose armaments because of their faith in the Socialist International, in which the German party was the largest single element. Successive congresses of the International had pledged the parties in the various countries to agitate against war, and Keir Hardie in 1910 attempted to secure the acceptance of a proposal for an international general strike in the event of hostilities. Although this proposal was rejected by the congress largely at the instance of the Germans who could see that it would prove impracticable, many Socialists retained a vague belief that somehow or other the International would be able to play a part in the prevention of a major war.

Inside the Labour Party, the discussion of foreign affairs was usually left to the Socialists : the trade-union members rarely worried their heads about it. But when it came to voting against the naval and military estimates, there were some who did not follow the majority of the party. The naval estimates, for instance, were supported by Labour M.P.s representing dockyard constituencies, as they did not want to be accused of depriving their constituents of much-needed employment. As a Conservative M.P. rather unkindly pointed out, 'I have noticed when members of the Labour Party happen to represent a dockyard constituency or a district in which armaments are created that there are no greater jingoes in the House'.[8] In addition, Will Thorne, who was a member of the S.D.F., believed like the other members of that organisation in a form of conscription known as 'the citizen army', which was based on the idea that a revolution could best be effected when all members of the working class had some training in the use of arms.

In general, however, the realities of Britain's diplomatic and military commitments made little impact upon the Labour Party. Nor was the party very much to blame for this : fearful of hostile reaction among their own supporters, Asquith and Grey took care not to reveal the nature of the military and naval agreements made with France. The result was an absence of informed discussion on one of the most vital topics of the day. Under the circumstances, it can be readily understood how it was that the Labour Party failed to come to grips with the real issues involved.

(4)

There is no doubt that many of the difficulties of the party in this period derived from its close association with the Liberals in the 1906 election. Although the electoral agreement had paid immediate dividends, there were long-term liabilities for the Labour Party which perhaps only Herbert Gladstone had fully appreciated. A party which had set out to represent a whole social class had become identified with the sectional interests of Liberalism — with Free Trade, Nonconformity, and Home Rule. The accession of the miners' M.P.s in 1909 only increased the tendency, for the miners' leaders of this period were much less militant than the leaders of other unions. The necessity of supporting the Liberal Government during the difficult years when the Osborne Judgment was in operation completed the subordination of the Parliamentary Labour Party to the position of 'handmaiden of Liberalism'.

Yet the parliamentary party was only part of a larger whole — the labour movement. The future of the parliamentary party lay to a very large extent with the trade unions and Socialist societies and perhaps even more with the local L.R.C.s or Labour Parties that began to grow up in the constituencies. A comparison of the official figures of membership of the party in 1906 and 1914 shows that considerable growth had taken place in all these categories. In 1914 the trade-union membership had fallen back as a result of the Osborne Judgment, but it was still over 1½ million, whereas in 1906 it had been only about 900,000. The affiliated membership of the Socialist societies — that is, the I.L.P. and the very much smaller Fabian Society — had grown from less than 17,000 to about 33,000 ; and the B.S.P. was applying to rejoin. Even more striking, however, was the growth of the party's local organisations. By 1915, no less than eighty-five trades councils were affiliated, and there were also some seventy-three local Labour Parties. There was some overlapping of political function between local Labour Parties and trades councils, and in a few towns both were recorded as being affiliated to the national Labour Party. But in 1906 there had been only eighty-three of both types of organisation put together. These organisations, which in most cases secured affiliations both from local trade-union branches and from local branches of the Socialist societies, were especially important for strengthening the party's hold in the constituencies.

In other ways, too, the party was constantly developing its strength. It had a national agent and two full-time party agents for visiting the constituencies; it also paid subsidies towards the maintenance of twenty local agents. Moreover, the party's influence gradually extended into areas which in 1906 had been almost untouched. In Scotland, for instance, where a quite separate but very weak body called the Scottish Workers Representation Committee had existed, responsibility had been assumed by a Scottish Council of the Labour Party, which was much more successful. In addition, a London Labour Party for the metropolitan area was belatedly established in 1914 — a development that had been delayed by the grip of the S.D.F. and then the B.S.P. upon the London Trades Council, and the unwillingness of that body up till 1914 to regard the Labour Party with favour. There were, of course, already a number of local Labour Parties in London boroughs or constituencies. Municipal activity by local parties and trades councils was constantly expanding, though London was late in the movement, owing to the strength of the old Progressive alliance on the L.C.C. But the defeat of the Progressives in 1907, and the outside propaganda work of the Labour M.P.s when they were resident in London, enabled a Labour group to develop on the L.C.C. from 1910 onwards.

The increasing size of the extra-parliamentary party meant that one man could no longer effectively combine the secretaryship with major parliamentary duties. Ramsay MacDonald from 1906 to 1911 managed to be secretary of both the parliamentary and the extra-parliamentary party; but by 1910 he was an obvious candidate for the chairmanship of the parliamentary party and it was clear that he could not do justice both to this post and to his extra-parliamentary responsibilities. He seems to have genuinely wanted the chairmanship, because of a feeling that he alone could provide the necessary leadership (and leadership, of course, was something rather more than earlier chairmen had provided). In 1910 he wrote to Hardie: 'I do not care a dump about the chairmanship, but I do want the party to be led. . . . Let it be led to the devil if you like, but do not let it be the nerveless thing of the past session'.[9] The illness of George Barnes enabled him to take over the chairmanship at the beginning of 1911, and the following year he relinquished the secretaryship of the external organisation to Arthur Henderson.

Arthur Henderson, as a non-Socialist ex-Liberal, had always been rather suspect among the Socialists of the Labour Party. But he had developed a considerable degree of loyalty to the organisation, and as a former official of an old craft union — the Friendly Society of Ironfounders — he carried great influence with the union element in the party. As secretary of the party, he now decided to become a Socialist, which he did by joining the Fabian Society. How far this was a matter of conviction is perhaps doubtful; there were, in fact, organisational reasons for his action. MacDonald, as secretary of the Labour Party, was also secretary of the British Bureau of the Socialist International. If Henderson were not nominally a Socialist he could not take this post, and therefore a key position in the International would probably fall to the Marxist B.S.P. To prevent this happening, Henderson underwent a new political baptism, if not a conversion.

Hardie was now ageing rapidly and it became obvious that the two most important figures in the party were MacDonald and Henderson. MacDonald was successful in his aim of turning the chairmanship of the parliamentary party into an effective leadership (the use of the word 'leader', however, was still not accepted); but inevitably he lost his close links with the organisation in the constituencies. A certain testiness and insensitivity to criticism also made him many enemies. Henderson, on the other hand, rapidly matured in experience and gained great popularity. But there was little conflict between the two men. Henderson was content to regard MacDonald as by far the most suitable parliamentary spokesman, for he had a high regard for his abilities. Their co-operation provided the party with an effective working team, and this accounts for the re-election of MacDonald as chairman of the parliamentary party in each successive session from 1911 to the outbreak of war.

By 1914, then, the Labour Party was consolidating its influence in towns and industrial areas throughout Britain. It had little or no support in purely agricultural constituencies, but it was getting into a position from which it might be able to contest a much increased range of constituencies, instead of the mere fifty of 1906. In the first 1910 election it had seventy-eight candidates; in the second 1910 election, for obvious reasons, it dropped back to fifty-six. But it was equally obvious that at an election in 1914 or 1915 it would be able to contest a hundred or more seats. The 1903 agreement with the Liberals would then become a thing of the past. Much uncertainty remained, however, owing to the failure to solve the problem of Irish Home Rule. The Labour Party had been obliged to support the Liberals on this issue, but in the course of 1914 it looked as if the struggle would end only in civil war.

Suddenly, however, the political pattern was transformed by an external catalyst — that of war on the continent of Europe, in which Britain quickly became involved.

NOTES

1. At their meeting on 11 Feb. 1907. See *Labour Party Quarterly Circular*, Apr. 1907, p. 3.
2. Hardie to Glasier, 27 Dec. 1908, Glasier Papers.
3. W. J. Braithwaite, diary 28 July, 1911, quoted in his *Lloyd George's Ambulance Wagon* (1957), p. 196.

4. I.L.P. *Annual Report,* 1910, p. 58.
5. Leonard Hall, *et al., Let Us Reform the Labour Party* (1910), p. 3.
6. MacDonald to Master of Elibank, 4 Oct. 1911, quoted Frank Owen, *Tempestuous Journey* (1954), pp. 207 f.
7. Hansard, *Parliamentary Debates,* ser. 5, xxvi, 725.
8. Quoted W. P. Maddox, *Foreign Relations in British Labour Politics* (Cambridge, Mass., 1934), p. 209.
9. MacDonald to Hardie, 1 Feb. 1910, Hardie Papers.

FURTHER READING

Except for the volume by G. D. H. Cole mentioned at the end of Chapter I, there is as yet no narrative of Labour Party history in this period. The book by W. P. Maddox, cited above, provides valuable analysis of policy formation within the party. W. S. Adams makes some interesting suggestions in his article 'Lloyd George and the Labour Movement' in *Past and Present,* 3 (1953), pp. 55-62. In addition, some biographies — *e.g.* Godfrey Elton, *Life of James Ramsay MacDonald* (1939) — and some memoirs — *e.g.* Philip Snowden, *Autobiography,* i (1934) — are useful. For the 'labour unrest', see G. D. H. Cole, *Short History of the British Working Class Movement* (new ed., 1948); for Syndicalism and Guild Socialism, see Alexander Gray, *The Socialist Tradition* (1946), chs. xv and xvi; for the S.D.F. and B.S.P. see C. Tsuzuki, *H. M. Hyndman and British Socialism* (1961).

CHAPTER III

Henderson's Party : War and Reconstruction
(1914–22)

(1)

ALTHOUGH the Labour Party had by no means ignored questions of foreign policy before July 1914, it was only with the outbreak of war that they became of paramount importance. From then onwards until 1918 and indeed in the early post-war years, up to 1922, issues of war and diplomacy were dominant in the party's councils.

As the Sarajevo crisis reached its climax at the end of July, the Labour Party took a vigorous share in the agitation against war which was sponsored throughout Europe by the Socialist International. On Sunday 1st August Germany declared war on Russia ; and next day Keir Hardie and Arthur Henderson took part in a mass demonstration in Trafalgar Square, urging the government to keep out. On Monday 3rd August Germany declared war on France ; and that morning the Parliamentary Labour Party met and decided to oppose British intervention when the Commons debated the question in the afternoon. Consequently, although Sir Edward Grey made an impassioned appeal for aid to France, and although he was supported not only by the Conservatives but also by the Irish Nationalists, Ramsay MacDonald sounded a discordant note by registering his party's disapproval. MacDonald's speech, significantly enough, was in large part an appeal to the rank and file of the Liberal Party. 'Whatever may happen,' he declared,

> whatever may be said about us, we will take the action
> . . . of saying that this country ought to have remained

neutral, because in the deepest parts of our hearts we believe that that was right and that that alone was consistent with the honour of our country and the traditions of the Party that are now in office.[1]

But Grey's speech and, more particularly, the invasion of Belgium which took place next day (4th August) had the effect of transforming public opinion. It now became clear that there was almost universal enthusiasm for the declaration of war, and many of those who had previously hesitated were convinced by the need to fight on behalf of Belgium, whether for the sake of honour or for reasons of national expediency. The British ultimatum to Germany expired late in the evening of 4th August; and next morning, when the National Executive of the Labour Party met, it was apparent that the party no longer presented a united front of opposition to the war. The resolution that it passed, and which was then endorsed at a joint meeting with the parliamentary party, was clearly a compromise. It deplored the fact that British support had been committed to France 'without the knowledge of our people', but it did not express direct opposition to the war, merely saying that it was the duty of the labour movement to 'secure peace at the earliest possible moment on such conditions as will provide the best opportunities for the re-establishment of amicable feelings between the workers of Europe'.[2] The vagueness of this statement shows that it was designed to hide serious differences. The fact was that only the I.L.P. leaders were advocating a downright opposition to the war, on the lines of their campaign against the South African War. The majority of Labour M.P.s felt that they must support the war effort now that hostilities had begun. They were encouraged in this view by the break-up of the façade of unity among continental Socialists, as the French and Belgian leaders called for resistance to the German invaders, and the German Social-Democratic M.P.s voted war credits for the Kaiser's armies.

Under these circumstances, Ramsay MacDonald found

it necessary to resign the leadership of the parliamentary party. The actual issue was the party's attitude to the supplementary estimates moved by the Prime Minister on 6th August, notice of which was given the previous day. At a meeting late on the 5th, the party decided not to oppose these estimates, and MacDonald thereupon resigned. Arthur Henderson was appointed to take his place, and soon the great majority of the Labour Party under Henderson's lead was supporting the government, taking part in a recruiting campaign and accepting an electoral truce for the duration of the war. MacDonald and most of his I.L.P. colleagues found themselves fighting a lonely battle against the war with the help of a small minority of Liberals. For propaganda against the war, MacDonald joined with four anti-war Liberals, Norman Angell, E. D. Morel, Charles Trevelyan, and Arthur Ponsonby, to form in September 1914 a body called the Union of Democratic Control. The U.D.C. demanded democratic control of foreign policy, no annexations, an international organisation to maintain peace, and disarmament. New alignments thus cut across the ranks of the Labour Party, and threatened its continued existence as a political force.

Yet at the time, there were few who thought that the war would last as long as a year. Although Henderson had disagreed with MacDonald and had taken his place as party chairman, he did not want to expel the anti-war minority from membership of the party, for he expected an early return to the peace-time condition of politics. The analogy of the Liberal Party's toleration of internal disagreements during the South African War, and its speedy recovery of unity and rise to power afterwards, must have been present in many minds. Furthermore, MacDonald and Henderson at least could still agree in condemning Grey's conduct of pre-war diplomacy; and it was significant that Henderson became a member, albeit an inactive member, of the U.D.C. In practice it proved possible for all sections of the labour movement to collaborate in seeking measures to safeguard living standards in the changed circumstances of war. As early as 5th August a War Emergency Workers' National Committee had been set up at a joint conference of labour and socialist organisations which had been summoned by Arthur Henderson in his capacity as Secretary of the Labour Party. The Workers' National Committee included both supporters and opponents of the war, for they found plenty of common ground on such issues as war-time unemployment, inflation, and profiteering.

As the war dragged on into 1915, however, collaboration between the different sections of the movement was subjected to increasing strain. In May 1915 Arthur Henderson was invited to join the First Coalition under Asquith. He referred the matter to the parliamentary party, which by a tiny majority was opposed to taking office; but the National Executive favoured it, and the issue was resolved by a joint meeting of the Executive and the parliamentary party, at which the majority of the latter were overruled. The difference of attitude of the two bodies may be explained by the greater strength of the I.L.P. in Parliament. Henderson then became President of the Board of Education, a somewhat unsuitable post, but with a seat in the Cabinet; and two other Labour M.P.s took junior office.

The influence of the Labour Party upon the actual conduct of government was not very noticeable at first. It seemed rather that the party was a prisoner of the other parties, obliged to take responsibility for various measures that were bound to be unpopular in the labour movement. One highly controversial issue was the dilution of labour in the factories — that is, the admission of unskilled workers into occupations hitherto reserved for craftsmen who had served their apprenticeship. Another was military conscription, which was strongly opposed by most sections of the labour movement. Members of the government soon began to realise that the participation of Henderson and his colleagues in office did not guarantee the loyalty of all the workers in the factories and mines. There was much industrial unrest, particularly on Clydeside; and early in 1916, when the conscription bill was being debated, the annual conference of the Labour Party went on record as opposed to the principle, although it coupled this with an indication that the party would cease to agitate the question if the bill was passed.

Lloyd George as Minister of Munitions had had direct experience of the importance of conciliating labour; and when in December 1916 he formed a government to replace that of Asquith he found it convenient to offer the Labour Party considerably better terms than before for its participation in the government. In fact, he gave an interview to 'a very representative attendance of both the Executive and the Parliamentary Party', at which he gave various undertakings about his policy and the part that he would enable Labour to play in the government. He promised state control of the mines and of shipping, and the introduction of an effective system of food rationing. This offer was too good to refuse; and so members of the Labour Party were authorised to enter the government again. Henderson this time was in a small War Cabinet of five members, and two other Labour M.P.s, John Hodge and George Barnes, became Minister of Labour and Minister of Pensions respectively, both of these ministries being new creations. Several other Labour M.P.s were appointed to junior posts.

At the beginning of 1917, therefore, there seemed to be a particularly deep cleavage between the Labour Party majority, which was so fully committed to Lloyd George's 'Win the War' government, and the I.L.P. minority, many of whose younger members were resisting the call-up and being taken away to military detention. It was significant that at the annual conference of the Labour Party in January a move was made to exclude the influence of the Socialist societies from the National Executive. It was proposed by union representatives, and carried by a narrow majority against the advice of Henderson, that the Executive members should all be elected by vote of the whole conference. This decision broke up the existing federal structure of the party, whereby both the Socialist societies and the trade unions elected their separate representatives; and it inevitably meant trade-union nomination of the entire body. The I.L.P. leaders naturally found it particularly obnoxious, and they began to talk of leaving the party. 'I am not going to sneak about', wrote MacDonald,

> and bargain for Trade Union votes for I.L.P. candidates for the Executive. . . . If a split were to come owing to the oppressive use of the block vote of some of the larger unions, I would do what I could to form a new Labour combination for political purposes.[3]

As it happened, however, — or was this Henderson's deliberate stage-management? — the proposal had only come up after the election of the Executive members for the following year; and by 1918, as we shall see, the political situation had entirely changed, so that the use of the block vote became far from 'oppressive', at least in the sense that MacDonald wished to imply.

(2)

The main changes that took place in the political climate in 1917 were due to the two revolutions in Russia and to the entry of the United States into the war. The first Russian Revolution was greeted with great enthusiasm on the Left, as was shown by the success of a special conference at Leeds in June, summoned by the United Socialist Council. This body was an unofficial body so far as the Labour Party was concerned, but it was really the joint voice of the I.L.P. and the B.S.P., which were both now affiliated to the Labour Party. The conference was attended by over a thousand delegates from local Socialist branches, from trade-union branches, and from trades councils. It expressed great gratification at the overthrow of Tsarism and saluted the prospect of a peace without annexations. It even urged the establishment of Soldiers' and Workmen's Councils in Britain, on the Russian model, but this was really more a gesture of sympathy for the Russians than a

ARTHUR HENDERSON (1863–1935)

carefully prepared move in the direction of a British revolution : it had almost no practical consequences.

What was significant, however, was the change of attitude of the trade-union rank and file, which was also reflected in the official leadership of the Labour Party itself. At the suggestion of Lloyd George, who wanted to keep Russia in the war, Henderson was sent to visit Russia ; and on his return he announced himself of the opinion that the best way to keep the Russians in line with the Western Allies was to explore in conjunction with them the basis for a negotiated peace.

Henderson also favoured the despatch of delegates from Britain to a proposed International Socialist Congress at Stockholm, which it was expected that German Socialists would attend. Further, he persuaded a special conference of the Labour Party to agree with him. This, however, precipitated a crisis with his colleagues in the War Cabinet. Summoned to a meeting of this body, of which he had been a member since the government was formed, Henderson was kept outside the door while its other members discussed his position. He was then formally rebuked by Lloyd George and accordingly resigned in a state of great indignation. It was obvious that Lloyd George, who had originally been sympathetic to Henderson's views on relations with Russia, had had his hand forced by the other members of the Cabinet. The crisis, later known as the 'doormat incident', was not revealed to the public until a fortnight later ; and Lloyd George managed to soften its impact by at once replacing Henderson with another Labour Party member, George Barnes, and by bringing another Labour M.P., George Wardle, into the government. The affair was thus kept on a personal level between Henderson and the Prime Minister ; and the government retained the support of the Labour Party while refusing exit visas for the Stockholm Conference.

All the same, the 'doormat incident' proved to be a turning-point in the history of the Labour Party. From that time onwards, Henderson, who was still secretary of the party, began to devote himself largely to its affairs, not only shaping a major reorganisation of its structure, but also devising an alternative foreign policy to that of the government. Henderson's work thus prepared the party to undertake the responsibilities of leading the opposition in the event of a general election. The opportunity was obvious, owing to the completely divided state of the Liberal Party. Even Walter Hines Page, the American ambassador, who was no friend to labour, could see the implications of Henderson's policy : as he wrote to President Wilson in January 1918, 'The Labour Party is already playing for supremacy'. Henderson, unlike MacDonald, was quite willing to pick the brains of the intellectuals ; and by December 1917 Beatrice Webb could say that her husband Sidney, who was on the National Executive as the representative of the Fabian Society, had become 'the intellectual leader of the Labour Party'.[4]

The most important change, however, was in the attitude of both the leadership and the rank and file of the trade unions. Already before the war it was the Miners Federation and the Railwaymen which had become the most radical of the unions, and these organisations, led by Robert Smillie and J. H. Thomas respectively, now began to press for a more independent political policy both by the T.U.C. and by the Labour Party. In 1917 the Parliamentary Committee of the T.U.C., realising both its power and its opportunity, began to take an active part in shaping a new foreign policy — a decision that was welcomed by Henderson. Consequently, when Henderson, with the help of Sidney Webb and Ramsay MacDonald, drew up a 'Memorandum on War Aims' towards the end of 1917, they secured its approval by both the National Executive of the party and the Parliamentary Committee of the T.U.C. The Memorandum demanded the establishment of a League of Nations and of machinery for the mediation of international disputes ; international trusteeship of African colonies ; and international action to deal with economic problems such as the supply of raw materials.

These far-sighted recommendations alienated some extreme 'patriotic' union leaders, some of whom seceded from the party. But they won such an overwhelming endorsement from the unions as a whole that they had much influence in the world, both upon Lloyd George and upon President Wilson, who through various agents kept a close watch on the development of British opinion. Lloyd George soon afterwards made a statement on war aims to a conference of trade unionists, and although it was in studiously vague terms it seemed to show some Labour Party influence; and President Wilson's Fourteen Points, which were enunciated a few days later, followed the same lines.

Meanwhile Henderson with the aid of Sidney Webb had also been preparing a new draft constitution for the Labour Party. His object was to weld the Socialist and trade-union elements firmly together and to provide for the admission to full membership of people who were not trade unionists : middle-class people, for instance, and also women, who were shortly to get the vote. The new draft therefore arranged for the opening of the local Labour Parties to individual membership, so that it would no longer be necessary for the Labour Party supporter to secure his membership of the party through one of the affiliated Socialist societies or trade unions. The composition of the Executive was to be changed : out of a proposed total of twenty-one seats, no less than five were to be reserved for nominees of local Labour Parties and another four for women. The remaining seats would be available for the nominees of trade unions and Socialist societies, between whom no distinction now remained. In accordance with the resolution of the 1917 conference, the actual election to all seats on the Executive was to be done by the whole conference : the federal principle had thus been abandoned.

If the Executive was henceforth to be completely dominated by the union block vote, at least the Socialists were to gain by the party's adoption of a Socialist constitution. This was drafted by Sidney Webb, who produced the celebrated Clause Four of the 'Party Objects' which for the first time explicitly committed the party to a Socialist basis :

> To secure for the producers by hand and brain the full fruits of their industry, and the most equitable distribution thereof that may be possible, upon the basis of the common ownership of the means of production and the best obtainable system of popular administration and control of each industry or service.[5]

It was a striking demonstration of the leftward trend in the unions that this constitution was adopted in February 1918 with only one amendment of any importance — the addition of two more seats for the affiliated societies (in effect, for the trade unions), bringing the Executive to a total of twenty-three. Only the I.L.P. really disliked the changes, for it lost its guaranteed seats on the Executive and its influence was rivalled by that of the local Labour Parties.

Only four months later — in June 1918 — the party held another conference, the first under the new constitution. It adopted a policy statement drafted by Sidney Webb, *Labour and the New Social Order*, which was of great importance because it formed the basis of Labour Party policy for over thirty years — in fact, until the general election of 1950. It incorporated four principles, which were set out in the methodical fashion that was typical of the work of Sidney Webb and his wife, Beatrice. The first was the concept of the National Minimum, which the Webbs had advocated at the time of the Poor Law Commission of 1905–9, and which the Labour Party had been slowly working towards before the war. The National Minimum, according to the statement, meant a comprehensive policy of full employment with a minimum wage and a minimum standard of working conditions, together with a maximum working week of forty-eight hours. The second principle was the Democratic Control of Industry : here Webb emphasised the need for nationalisation of industry but also made somewhat vague concessions to the Guild Socialist standpoint which was now so popular among parts of the labour movement — particularly the Miners and the Railwaymen. The third principle was summed up as 'The Revolution in National Finance', which meant in practice the subsidisation of social services by heavy taxation of large incomes and, more specifically, an immediate capital levy to pay off a part of the cost of the war. Finally, the fourth principle was 'The Surplus for the Common Good', which proclaimed that the balance of the nation's wealth should so far as possible be devoted to expanding opportunities in education and in culture for the people as a whole.

The party was thus equipped with a greatly improved constitution, at least for the purpose of making an appeal to the electorate as a whole rather than just to the interest of the unions. It also had a practical programme which in domestic affairs was a compromise between Marxian Socialism on the one hand and the piecemeal social reform of the Chamberlain-Lloyd George type on the other. All this enabled the party to make its bid to rank as an alternative government of the country: a bid that within the first post-war years was to prove unexpectedly successful.

(3)

Meanwhile several members of the Parliamentary Labour Party had remained as members of the Lloyd George Coalition. When the war ended on 11th November, a decision had to be taken on the question of withdrawal from the government. The idea of withdrawal was not welcome to the ministers concerned: Barnes enjoyed being in the War Cabinet and was easily persuaded by Lloyd George of the need for Labour to take part in the post-war settlement; and Clynes, who had become Food Controller, was also happily engaged in administration. Consequently, the Parliamentary Labour Party mostly favoured remaining in office. But the National Executive under Henderson's influence took the opposite view, which was confirmed by a special Labour Party Conference on 14th November.

Clynes reluctantly obeyed the injunction to leave the government; but Barnes and others refused to resign and so forfeited their membership of the Labour Party.

The general election took place in December 1918, and was inevitably a virtual plebiscite for or against Lloyd George, as the architect of victory. In the face of heavy odds, the Labour Party put up a brave fight: it fielded 361 candidates — an enormous increase compared with its previous maximum of 78 in the first 1910 election. The divisions in the Liberal Party enabled the Labour Party to assume the position of chief opposition party in many constituencies; but the advantage of this situation was more for the future than for the immediate election, as the tide ran so strongly in favour of the Coalition candidates. In fact, Labour won only fifty-seven seats, which was not a very great improvement on its pre-war totals. It was more significant that in another seventy-nine constituencies where there were three or four candidates, the party ran second to the winner, and ahead of a Liberal. Henceforth, the onus of 'splitting the progressive vote' would lie upon the Liberals. This was especially important now that nearly all the two-member constituencies, which had enabled Liberal and Labour to run in harness, had been abolished by the 1918 Reform Act.

The misfortune of the Parliamentary Labour Party, however, was that for the time being it had lost all its ablest spokesmen. The I.L.P. leaders MacDonald and Snowden were defeated because of their anti-war record; and Arthur Henderson also lost his seat. Of the fifty-seven who found their way to Parliament, twenty-five were miners and twenty-four represented other unions; five were sponsored by local Labour Parties and only three by the I.L.P. Of the well-known leaders of the party, only Clynes survived; and when the parliamentary party met to choose its chairman, it re-elected the Scottish miner Willie Adamson, 'respectable but dull-witted' as Mrs. Webb described him,[6] who had acted as chairman just before the dissolution. It should be added that the Co-operative Union entered politics during the war, and sponsored several candidates, one of whom was elected. The one Co-operative M.P. joined the Parliamentary Labour Party, as did others after later elections; and the 'Co-operative Party' became closely integrated with the Labour Party.

The status of the Parliamentary Labour Party *vis-à-vis* the National Executive and the labour movement at large was now at its nadir. It was bad enough that several of the parliamentary leaders had refused to leave the Coalition Government; it was worse still that the party in the House had lost its remaining members of ability, and that even Henderson, who had so ably conducted the work of re-organisation, had failed to secure re-election. This was just at a moment when the party's revised constitution and policy were beginning to win it an increasing number of middle-class recruits. The demand for a peace without annexations, for instance — the old demand of the U.D.C. — brought to the party many of the able young Liberals who had opposed the war and had then despaired of their own divided party. In more senses than one, they were a 'Foreign Legion' as they were dubbed at the time by one of their own number.[7]

At the same time, it had become obvious that the parliamentary leaders had won their place in the Coalition not because of their numbers in the House but because of the strength of the industrial movement with which they were linked. The readiness of the T.U.C. and of the unions to participate in various types of political action, which became evident for the first time in 1917, remained after the end of the war, and expanded into a threat of direct industrial action for political ends. The most striking example of this was the pressure brought to bear by the T.U.C. in 1920 to secure a termination of British intervention against the Bolsheviks. A Council of Action was set up after the London Dockers, encouraged by their leader Ernest Bevin, had taken the initiative in refusing to load a ship called the *Jolly George* until munitions on board, which were destined for Poland, had been removed. There is more than a possibility that this boycott and the threat of further action played a major part in altering Lloyd George's policy and so preventing further British intervention. But it was, of course, unconstitutional action which by-passed Parliament and did nothing to enhance the credit of the Parliamentary Labour Party.

The early post-war period was marked by much industrial unrest and trade-union militancy. This was partly because economic conditions were bad — for an immediate post-war boom, coupled with considerable inflation, collapsed suddenly in 1920 into a slump and heavy unemployment. But it was also because the ideas of 'direct action' in vogue just before the war were still widely current among union leaders. In particular, the 'triple alliance' of the Miners, Railwaymen, and Transport Workers, which had been formed just before the war with the object of securing united pressure against their employers, had not yet been put to the test. The idea of a General Strike was also in the air, the miners urging that it would be the best way of securing the nationalisation of the mines which was now their immediate goal.

Unfortunately for the miners, however, even the 'triple alliance' proved unreliable. Like similar alliances in the wider field of international diplomacy, it depended at every test upon the self-interest of each of its components; and in April 1921, on a day known thereafter as 'Black Friday', it broke up when the other unions refused to continue their support for the miners in a strike threat. It came to be recognised that the only way to bring effective joint industrial pressure to bear was to have a unified command of the unions like the General Staff of an army. Consequently, in the course of 1921 the old Parliamentary Committee of the T.U.C., which had been little more than an agency for lobbying the older political parties at Westminster, was transformed into a General Council with greater powers to co-ordinate policy — though not, in the last resort, to order the unions about unless they conceded emergency powers to it. Henceforth the General Council assumed an important political as well as industrial role, building up a headquarters staff which rivalled that of the Labour Party; and it was noteworthy that the ablest union leaders preferred to serve on the General Council rather than to go into what must have seemed the comparative backwater of parliamentary politics. The Labour Party did its best to maintain liaison with the new organisation: for this purpose a National Joint Council was set up, consisting of representatives of the General Council, the Parliamentary Labour Party, and the party's National Executive.

(4)

In the first post-war years, parliamentary politics had little importance for the party as a whole. Although Henderson was returned to the Commons in a by-election in 1919, he did not attempt to resume the chairmanship, preferring to occupy himself in the task of extending extra-parliamentary organisation. In 1920 the obviously incompetent Adamson was succeeded as chairman by Clynes, an abler if not exactly dashing figure. But Henderson held the initiative with his external activities, such as the special Labour Party Commission of Enquiry sent to Ireland to investigate the outrages of the 'Black and Tans'. This did not mean, however, that Henderson had lost interest in parliamentary action; it simply indicated that he was biding his time until a new general election should strengthen the party's representation in the Commons.

The fundamentally constitutional and law-abiding attitude of Henderson and his colleagues was indicated clearly by their reaction to the Communist Party's application for affiliation in 1920. The Communist Party had been formed that year, by the amalgamation of the old B.S.P. and various other smaller left-wing groups on a basis of support for the Russian Bolsheviks. The B.S.P. had been affiliated to the Labour Party since 1916, and it might have seemed natural for the new party also to have secured affiliation as a Socialist society. But the National Executive rejected the application on the ground that the Communist aims were not in accord with the 'constitution, principles, and programme' of the Labour Party.[8] The decision was an indication of the hardening discipline of the party as well as of its hostility to extreme revolutionary tactics. The decision of the Executive was endorsed by a large majority at the 1921 Labour Party Conference.

In 1922 came a new general election and with it the reward for the skilful generalship of Henderson in the preceding eight years. The party increased the number of seats that it contested to 414, which was now over two-thirds of the total. It won altogether 142 of them — almost double its strength at the dissolution, which had already been recruited by successes at by-elections. Although there was a clear Conservative majority in Parliament, in many ways the rise of the Labour Party to a total exceeding that of the broken segments of the Liberal Party was the most important single feature of the election. Furthermore, the new Parliamentary Labour Party contained all the abler leaders of the party, with the very temporary exception of Henderson who had the bad luck again to be defeated (he came in at a by-election in January 1923). Although there were now eighty-five trade-union nominees — which was a considerable increase — it was much more noteworthy that the candidates sponsored by the I.L.P. had won thirty-two seats, as against three in 1918, and that these included not only the anti-war M.P.s such as Mac-Donald and Snowden but also various men of good education such as Clement Attlee and Dr. Alfred Salter. The I.L.P. was also especially successful in Scotland: it won nine seats in Glasgow alone, and the Scottish I.L.P. formed a militant group which was distinctly to the left of the older leaders. In fact, they were the political offspring of the industrial discontent of wartime, which in Scotland had assumed the form of a national movement. In England, the gains made were less distinctively made by the I.L.P.: the Labour Party did, however, win strength in areas where before the war it had been comparatively weak in the face of Liberalism: notably in Yorkshire and the North-East, and in Greater London. Thus in its success it assumed a more general and national character than before, with M.P.s from all classes of the community — a fitting prelude to its assumption of the role of His Majesty's Opposition.

NOTES

1. Hansard, *Parliamentary Debates*, ser. 5, lxv, 1831.
2. *Labour Party Annual Report*, 1916, pp. 3 f.
3. *Forward*, 10 Feb. 1917, quoted C. T. Solberg, 'The Independent Labour Party, 1893 to 1918' (Oxford B.Litt. thesis), p. 198.
4. Diary, 11 Dec. 1917, M. I. Cole (ed.), *Beatrice Webb's Diaries, 1912–1924* (1952), p. 99.
5. *Labour Party Seventeenth Annual Report*, 1918, p. 140.
6. M. I. Cole, *op. cit.* p. 141.
7. George Young, quoted Maddox, *Foreign Relations in British Labour Politics*, p. 74.
8. Henderson to Inkpin, 11 Sept. 1920, quoted in *Labour Party Annual Report*, 1921, p. 19.

FURTHER READING

G. D. H. Cole's *History of the Labour Party from 1914* (1948) provides much information for the whole period up to its publication date. More detailed work on the war and early post-war years has tended to concentrate on matters of foreign policy, and here we are particularly indebted to American scholars: W. P. Maddox, for the book already cited; Carl F. Brand, *British Labour's Rise to Power* (Stanford, Calif., 1941); and Stephen R. Graubard, *British Labour and the Russian Revolution* (Cambridge, Mass., 1956). A. J. P. Taylor, *The Trouble Makers* (1957), contains an interesting account of the Union of Democratic Control. See also Henry Pelling, *America and the British Left* (1956), ch. vii. M. A. Hamilton's *Arthur Henderson* (1938) is not without merit, but lacks documentation. It may be supplemented by M. I. Cole (ed.), *Beatrice Webb's Diaries, 1912–1924* (1952) — the most valuable section of the diaries for Labour Party history. V. L. Allen, 'Re-organisation of the T.U.C., 1918–27', *British Journal of Sociology*, xi (1960), 24-43, is helpful on an allied subject.

CHAPTER IV

The MacDonald Leadership
(1922-31)

(1)

THE years 1922-31 were the years of Ramsay MacDonald's leadership of the Labour Party. The very concept of 'leadership' was something of a novelty: but MacDonald was a leader in a sense that none of his predecessors in the party chairmanship (including himself before the war) had been. From 1922 he was described as not just the 'chairman' of the parliamentary party but as its 'chairman and leader'. The phrase was used to indicate that he was also Leader of the Opposition and potential Prime Minister. The fact that the parliamentary party had established its right to be regarded as the official Opposition in the Commons meant additional prestige and importance for its principal spokesman, who now became the prospective dispenser of government patronage. Similarly, the parliamentary party as a whole considerably increased its standing *vis-à-vis* the trade unions.

MacDonald's elevation by the parliamentary party in place of the incumbent, J. R. Clynes, was a remarkable success, and it could not have happened if the 1922 general election had not completely transformed the character of the parliamentary party. The great change was the increase in the number of Labour M.P.s who were not sponsored by the unions. As we have seen, many of the newcomers were I.L.P. members, and not a few were former Liberals of the U.D.C. type. For them — even for the very militant Clydeside I.L.P.ers — MacDonald had long worn the martyr's crown as the principal opponent of the war. The

Clydeside men were soon to regret their choice, because of
the very moderate tone of MacDonald's domestic policies.
But by then it was too late : for the 'leader' as he had
become benefited from the sturdy loyalty of the trade
unionists, who gave him the same trust as they themselves
would have expected from the rank and file of a trade
union during an industrial strike.   The example was set by
Henderson and by Clynes himself, who both recognised
MacDonald's exceptional parliamentary abilities and served
him without rancour.

MacDonald was fully conscious of the character of his
task, and of the fact that he was in a completely different
position from any earlier chairman of the parliamentary
party.   Writing to an American friend, he compared his
role to that of former Conservative or Liberal Leaders of
the Opposition :

> My real difficulty is that with a very small income
> I have stepped into a job that has never been filled before
> by anyone who had not a command of much money;
> and also that whereas my predecessors inherited secre-
> taries and a going machine, I inherited nothing and am
> having to make everything.[1]

Meanwhile the configuration of the extra-parliamentary
party was changing all the time.   There were certain formal
changes that operated in the direction of increasing the
party's discipline and acceptance of leadership from above.
The *Herald*, which had been restored as a daily in 1919
and had continued to be a journal of the Left, in 1922 for
financial reasons fell under the control of the Labour Party
and the T.U.C., and the left-wing George Lansbury ceased
to be editor.   At the same time the Communist Party with
financial help from Moscow emerged as a highly disciplined
group on the Left demanding still more insistently to be
admitted to affiliation to the Labour Party; and when this
was refused, its members attempted to infiltrate and win
control of the local Labour Parties.   The National Executive found it necessary to respond to this pressure by a

tightening of discipline. By decisions of the party conferences of 1922 to 1925 it ensured that Communists were
debarred from individual membership of the party and from
selection as its parliamentary candidates, although they
could still attend annual conferences as union delegates.
By 1925, however, the Communists and their sympathisers
had already managed to 'capture' quite a number of the
local parties, especially the still rather feeble ones in the
London area; and by the summer of 1927 the National
Executive had had to disaffiliate a total of 23, including 15
in the London area. These rebellious parties were organised by the Communists as a 'National Left Wing Movement'; but this body was outside the Labour Party, and
the expelled local parties were promptly replaced by new
ones formed by the National Executive.

There were, however, certain other changes which went
far to neutralise the increase in formal discipline. One was
the increasing tendency of the major trade-union leaders,
owing to pressure of work, to concentrate their efforts on
the industrial side of the movement and to ignore the
Labour Party. As we have seen, it was now rare for the
secretary of a large trade union to sit in Parliament; and
membership of the General Council was considered to be
incompatible with membership of the National Executive of
the Labour Party. Furthermore, at least one very large
union, the new Transport and General Workers, which had
been created out of the old dockers' unions by Ernest
Bevin, began to regard the House of Commons as nothing
more than a convenient place of retirement for redundant
officials.[2] Such an attitude to parliamentary politics had
an unfavourable effect, not only upon the quality of the
trade-union contribution to the Labour Party, but also
upon the degree of effective co-ordination between the two
sides of the labour movement.

Another centrifugal tendency was apparent in the gradual
evolution of the I.L.P. away from its old position as the
reconciler of unionism and Socialism. The organisation
had not yet suffered any great loss of membership as a

result of the expansion of the role of the local Labour Parties; but it had suffered a change of character. It had become something of a 'cave of Adullam' for Socialists who were impatient with the conservatism of the party's leaders. This characteristic had of course begun to develop on questions of foreign policy during the war years; but with the post-war alternative of individual membership in a local Labour Party, it became apparent that those who deliberately chose to join the I.L.P. were those who wanted a more Socialist and possibly Marxist policy than would be provided by the Henderson-Webb formulae. Even the thorough-going Marxists, unless they were Communists, had to join the I.L.P., now that the old British Socialist Party had disappeared. Leadership for these left-wing Socialists was provided by the Clydesiders, among whom James Maxton was the most prominent; but up till 1924 the old association of MacDonald with the growth of the I.L.P., and the memory of his role during the war, muted any tendency of Maxton and his friends to attack their parliamentary leader, especially so soon after they had played a major part in his selection.

At the end of 1923 Stanley Baldwin, the new Conservative Prime Minister, suddenly dissolved Parliament on the Tariff Reform issue, and a general election ensued. The Labour Party was taken by surprise by these events, but it managed to raise a few more candidates than in 1922, and in an election which swung against the Conservatives (for Tariff Reform was still generally unpopular in Britain) it gained considerably from its position as the larger opposition party in most constituencies. Consequently, although the reunited Liberal Party much improved its position and won 158 seats, the Labour Party also ran further ahead up to a total of 191 seats. The fresh victories were won in areas where the party had remained unusually weak even in 1922: in London alone 15 seats were gained. The I.L.P.-sponsored M.P.s numbered 39, as against 32 in 1922; those sponsored by local Labour Parties increased from 19 to 39. The total of these two — 78 — was beginning to compare with the total trade-union representation, which had moved up merely from 85 to 101.

The Conservatives, with 258 members, were still the largest party in the Commons, but they had no clear majority. As the election had largely been fought on Tariff Reform, which the electorate had rejected, it was clearly the duty of the parties advocating Free Trade to form a government between them, and the Liberals decided to support a Labour Government. In January 1924, therefore, the King called upon MacDonald to form a ministry.

(2)

In choosing his Cabinet, MacDonald at once showed that, while he had plenty of confidence in his own abilities, he did not think very much of his colleagues in the party. He acted as his own Foreign Secretary, and for the offices of Lord President, Lord Chancellor, and First Lord of the Admiralty he went outside the party, bringing in Lord Haldane, the former Liberal minister, Lord Parmoor, a former Conservative M.P., and Lord Chelmsford, also a Conservative. Snowden went to the Exchequer, and Clynes became Lord Privy Seal and Deputy Leader in the Commons. MacDonald tried to keep Henderson out altogether, apparently on the grounds that the ministry would not last long and that Henderson having been defeated (as usual) in the general election could best engage in preparing the party machinery for another contest. But Henderson would not accept this rebuff and insisted on a senior Cabinet post : he obtained the Home Office. The new I.L.P. Left was represented only by John Wheatley, a Clydesider, who became Minister of Health; but the gentle Fred Jowett of Bradford, a left-of-centre I.L.P. member of the older generation, became First Commissioner of Works. On the whole, the trade-union representation was comparatively small — but it was true that there were few suitable trade-union candidates for office.

The new government depended, of course, upon the

GEORGE LANSBURY (1859–1940)

support of the Liberals: the possibility of introducing any sort of Socialist programme was therefore out of the question. But it is doubtful if Snowden, as Chancellor of the Exchequer, actually wanted to do anything of which the most orthodox Liberal would have disapproved. His budget, from the Liberal standpoint, was unimpeachable: he cut taxes for both rich and poor. Few of the so-called economic experts of the Labour Party realised the need for a policy of expansion and public works to deal with the prevailing unemployment. For the most part, they saw no remedy short of 'Socialism' which, as they very well knew, could not be attained in the foreseeable future.

There was, however, one modest success for the Labour Government in the domestic sphere. This was Wheatley's Housing Act. This measure, passed of course with Liberal support, provided for government aid in building council houses. Under the Act, a good deal of building was initiated, and this had a stimulating effect on the economy, though most of the effect came only in the later years of the decade when the Conservatives were again in office. It was an interesting fact that the one minister to distinguish himself as a master of the difficult art of securing social legislation in a minority government, was the one representative of the new I.L.P. Left in the Cabinet.

But by far the greatest success of the government was in foreign policy. Here, of course, the government could act more independently of Parliament, and MacDonald soon justified his decision to be his own Foreign Minister. Faced by the problem of Franco-German enmity, which had culminated in the French occupation of the Ruhr, MacDonald now made a friendly approach to Poincaré, the French Premier. This was a move as shrewd as it was surprising, for MacDonald might have been expected to take a very anti-French line on the basis of his known attitude to the war and to the Versailles Treaty. Poincaré responded in a friendly fashion, and Anglo-French accord became even closer when Poincaré's government fell and Herriot took over. A conference was held in London to secure the acceptance of the Dawes Plan, whereby an American loan was to underwrite German reparations; and the success of the conference undoubtedly owed much to MacDonald's diplomacy, although it involved an acceptance by the Labour Government of the principle of reparations.

MacDonald's attitude to the League of Nations was at first somewhat ambivalent, for he did not like the fact that the League had originated in the Treaty of Versailles. But he did take the trouble to attend a meeting of the League Assembly at Geneva in September, and he encouraged Henderson and Parmoor to work out a draft treaty for real collective security, in collaboration with representatives of other powers. This draft became known as the Geneva Protocol. Whether a Labour Government would ever have ratified the Protocol, with its commitments to assist in keeping the peace in Europe, is perhaps doubtful: Henderson and Parmoor approved it, of course, but MacDonald seemed lukewarm. The fall of the government, however, left the onus of its rejection to the Conservatives.

There was one further major issue in foreign affairs. This was the question of Anglo-Russian relations. The government made a start by giving unconditional recognition to the Soviet Government; but it proved much more difficult to agree on the terms of financial and commercial agreements. The talks between the Soviet emissaries and the Foreign Office actually broke down and were only resumed as a result of the intervention of a group of Labour M.P.s. This gave the Conservatives an opportunity to argue that the government had given way to left-wing pressure, and a strong anti-Soviet propaganda ensued, which had its effect upon the Liberals.

It was really this issue which brought the government down, although the actual incident which provoked the parliamentary crisis was a trivial matter of domestic politics. J. R. Campbell, the acting editor of a small Communist journal, had published an article urging soldiers not to 'turn your guns on your fellow workers' in industrial disputes. The Attorney-General, Sir Patrick Hastings, decided that this was seditious and a prosecution was initiated. Later on, however, he changed his mind and withdrew the prosecution. The Conservatives, scenting left-wing interference with the judicial process, secured a debate on this issue when the House met in October. Although Hastings effectively answered the charges, MacDonald's defence was unsatisfactory — he had been too absorbed in problems of foreign policy — and a combination of Conservative and Liberal votes defeated the government on a demand for a Select Committee. MacDonald decided to dissolve Parliament and a new general election took place.

The 1924 general election was a notable victory for the Conservatives. Compared with 1923, they won an extra 155 seats. But the Labour Party on balance lost only 40 seats — a little over a fifth of their existing holding. The Liberals bore the brunt, losing 118 and being reduced to a total of 40 — little more than a quarter of the Labour total of 151. It is generally maintained that the Zinoviev letter scare, which took place in election week, significantly affected the polling; but if so, it is difficult to see why the Liberals suffered so heavily rather than the Labour Party. In fact, the Conservatives benefited considerably from their temporary abandonment of Tariff Reform, which won them votes from many who had previously voted Liberal. Consequently, although the Labour vote went up by half a million, it could not keep up with the Conservative success.

On the whole the first Labour Government had performed creditably; and the return of Labour's main opponent in the election was only to be expected after a period of minority rule. But MacDonald had taken too much onto his own shoulders, and he had made one or two errors of tactics, notably in dealing with the Campbell Case and the Zinoviev letter. He had also shown himself very hostile to criticism, particularly from the I.L.P. Both he and his ministers had also signally failed to maintain effective liaison with the T.U.C., and the machinery of the National Joint Council had hardly been used. Consequently, on the

morrow of the general election MacDonald's stock, and that
of the parliamentary party generally, had considerably sunk
within the movement as a whole.

(3)

It was in this situation that the political initiative began
to move to the trade-union leaders, who had still not
abandoned their hopes of 'direct action'. The General
Council had already been showing signs of increased militancy, partly owing to the resignation of some of its more
moderate members to join the Labour Government; and
in 1925 the Conservative Chancellor of the Exchequer,
Winston Churchill, indirectly gave a further impetus to
this tendency by putting the country back on the gold
standard, which led to a crisis in the coal export trade and
demands by the coal-owners for sharp reductions in miners'
wages. The miners invoked the aid of the General Council,
which in turn promised the support of the transport workers
to enforce an embargo on the movement of coal. Faced by
this threat, the government gave way in July and agreed
to subsidise miners' pay up to 1st May 1926, while a Royal
Commission enquired into the problems of the industry.
Although the government had made a concession in this
instance, it had no intention of doing so again: and it
used the intervening months to make preparations in case
1926 should bring a fresh challenge from the T.U.C.

The parliamentary party could do little in the face of
the impending industrial conflict. MacDonald knew that
if he ventured criticisms of the use of strike action for general
political objects, his views would only be indignantly brushed
aside by the trade-union militants. The miners were clearly
the victims of injustice, and as the other union leaders saw
it, their own role was simply a form of sympathetic action
to enable the miners to hold their position. The decision
to use industrial pressure for political ends was for most of
them a decision made unconsciously rather than consciously.

The nine days' General Strike of May 1926 need not be

recounted in detail here. It was, of course, a failure. The General Council, unlike the government, had made virtually no preparations for the struggle, and although the withdrawal of labour was almost complete in the industries concerned, a number of tactical errors were made in issuing the orders. For instance, it was a mistake to bring out the printers, as it allowed the government to maintain a monopoly of news by means of the wireless. Furthermore, the General Council had no means of enforcing its demands in the face of a resolute government, supported as it inevitably was by the great bulk of public opinion. When it became clear that the government would not yield and that essential supplies would be kept flowing, there was nothing that the leaders of the General Council could do ; and as the days passed they began to realise their dilemma, and became anxious to find almost any excuse to order a return to work. The result was that the strike ended in almost complete defeat, with the miners' dispute — its original cause — completely unresolved. The miners, who felt that they had been betrayed, stayed on strike for several months more, until they finally had to capitulate to the terms of the mine-owners. But the most important result of the General Strike for the rest of the labour movement was the very general recognition that industrial action on so wide a scale was little short of attempted revolution. The unions and their leaders in reality had no desire to by-pass the usual constitutional channels of government, and they did not try it again. Instead, they began to look once more upon the parliamentary party as the agent of their political struggles.

In the immediately following months, the parliamentary party could not do much more than fight a rearguard action in defence of the unions. The Conservatives, rather foolishly exploiting their victory, passed a Trade Disputes Act which retrospectively illegalised the General Strike and imposed the 'contracting-in' system on union members who wished to pay the political levy to the Labour Party. Owing to the apathy of union members in general, this considerably reduced the party's funds until its repeal in 1946.

With the union leadership abandoning its erstwhile militancy, it might have been supposed that the Communist Party would gain supporters among the rank and file; but in fact its success was very limited, although its backing of the miners' cause in the latter months of 1926 won it a few thousand temporary recruits. In 1928 its hard-won gains in the National Left Wing movement and its influence on members of the Labour Party through other propaganda organisations was largely thrown away by a sudden switch of policy adopted on orders of the Communist International in Moscow. The new policy was one of complete sectarianism, involving an abandonment of the 'united front' method of infiltrating the Labour Party, and resulting in a denunciation of both leaders and members of the Labour Party as 'Social Fascists'. Naturally this policy at once reduced Communist influence within the Labour Party to a negligible factor, and entirely prevented the Communist leaders from exploiting the errors and vicissitudes of the Labour Party in the succeeding four years.

The challenge to MacDonald's leadership offered by the I.L.P., however, was of an altogether different order. With a much larger membership and with a long tradition of leadership within the Labour Party — more than two-thirds of the members of the parliamentary party actually held I.L.P. membership — the behaviour of the I.L.P. was of much greater immediate importance. In 1927 the I.L.P. brought forward a new statement of policy, entitled 'Socialism in Our Time'. Its principal proposal was for the introduction by a Labour Government of a 'Living Wage' — a minimum wage which would help to stimulate consumption and so revitalise the national economy. In shaping this programme the I.L.P. had had the advice of J. A. Hobson, one of the ablest economists of the time and in many ways a Keynesian before Keynes. There was nothing particularly extreme about this: but now that the I.L.P. was led by Maxton and others who were equally given to uncompromising utterances, there was little chance of the new programme being accepted by the Labour Party as a whole. At the 1927 Labour Party Conference it was opposed not only by MacDonald and Snowden, with their rigidly orthodox economic ideas, but also by many of the trade-union leaders, who felt that it might in some way or other adversely affect their sectional interests.

It was at the 1927 conference that the I.L.P. made clear its disapproval of MacDonald, by refusing to nominate him for the post of Treasurer of the Labour Party which he had held since 1912. The following year the Labour Party conference adopted a rather vague policy statement called *Labour and the Nation*, which was in no way an advance and in some ways a retreat from the earlier statement, *Labour and the New Social Order*, prepared by Henderson and Webb in 1918. Thereafter, the rift between I.L.P. policy and Labour Party policy seemed unbridgeable, and a struggle ensued on the question of whether I.L.P.-sponsored M.P.s should support the policy of the I.L.P. or that of the Labour Party.

This conflict was unresolved when in 1929 the term of the Conservative Government drew towards its close and a new general election took place. The Labour Party benefited from the popular feeling of dissatisfaction with the existing economic situation, and especially the chronic unemployment. The party's M.P.s in the new House totalled 288, which made it for the first time the largest party, although still with no clear majority. Among the 288 there was an enormous increase in the total sponsored by divisional Labour Parties — 128 as against 25 in 1924. This was partly due to the weakness of the unions after the passing of the Trade Disputes Act, and partly to the secession from the I.L.P. of candidates who could not agree with its sectional attitude. But in addition, any general electoral swing towards Labour was likely to result in specially marked gains for the local Labour Parties, because their candidates, unlike those of the unions, tended to be concentrated in the marginal or unfavourable constituencies. For the first time, trade-union-sponsored M.P.s numbered less than half the total, being only 115 out of 288. I.L.P.-sponsored successes numbered 36, almost half of them being in Scotland, and the Co-operative Party won 9 seats. As for the geographical distribution of the party in general, considerable progress was again made in the London area, and the depression in the Lancashire cotton trade enabled it to win 39 seats there, as against 18 in 1924. The verdict of the electorate clearly was that the Labour Party should be allowed another attempt at government.

(4)

MacDonald's Cabinet included most of those who had served in 1924, although Haldane, on whom MacDonald had previously relied for details of procedure, had died in 1928. The new Cabinet was constructed in consultation with Thomas, the Railwaymen's leader, Snowden, and Henderson. Henderson insisted on the Foreign Office, and MacDonald conceded it somewhat reluctantly, having toyed with the idea of appointing the rather more pliant Thomas to the post. Snowden returned to the Exchequer and Thomas became Lord Privy Seal. Wheatley and Jowett, who were identified with the policy of the I.L.P., were both dropped, but Lansbury was taken in instead as a representative of the Left. An important novelty was that Thomas, assisted by a three-man committee, was appointed to draw up plans to deal with unemployment. The three assistants were Lansbury (whose department was the Office of Works), Thomas Johnston (Under-Secretary for Scotland), and Oswald Mosley (Chancellor of the Duchy of Lancaster).

MacDonald realised his own and his colleagues' weakness on economic affairs and in 1930 established an Economic Advisory Council, consisting of economists, industrialists, and others to advise him on economic problems. Unfortunately, the experts could not agree and Snowden preferred to follow the recommendations of his Treasury officials. Meanwhile, the unemployment figures continued to rise, and by the autumn of 1930 exceeded two million.

The only minister to demand action, even at the expense of his office, was Mosley, who proposed state control of foreign trade and the expansion of purchasing power in the home market. When this was not accepted, he resigned from the government, being replaced by Clement Attlee.

As in 1924, MacDonald's main interest was in diplomacy. Although Henderson was Foreign Secretary, the Prime Minister reserved for himself the control of naval disarmament negotiations and other matters which principally involved Anglo-American relations. The Washington Naval Treaty of 1922 was expiring, but there was difficulty in reaching a fresh agreement. On taking office, MacDonald at once cut the British naval building programme and then personally visited America to discuss the terms of a new treaty. This led to a five-power conference in London in January 1930, which resulted in agreed reductions in their forces by Britain, America, and Japan, though not by France and Italy. MacDonald also showed keen interest in the development of self-government in India, and took the responsibility for the Viceroy's declaration that 'Dominion status' was the goal of British policy there. After the report of the Simon Commission in 1930, a Round Table Conference on the future of India was summoned for the autumn of 1930, but it had to be adjourned early in 1931, largely owing to the refusal of the Indian National Congress to take part. MacDonald persevered, however, and arranged for a resumption in the autumn in the expectation that Congress delegates would then attend.

In other matters of foreign policy, Henderson was in charge. One of the distinctive things he did, at the instigation of his Under-Secretary, Hugh Dalton, was to distribute copies of *Labour and the Nation* to permanent officials in the Foreign Office. His main achievements were: a commercial treaty with Russia, following a resumption of diplomatic relations; the withdrawal of occupation forces from the Rhineland and a resumption of work on preparations for a general disarmament conference; the signature of the optional clause of the Statute for the Permanent

Court of International Justice, accepting compulsory arbitration in international disputes; and a complete change in policy towards Egypt, though falling short of an Anglo-Egyptian Treaty owing to difficulties about the status of the Sudan. Henderson's work laid the groundwork for effective international agreements on various outstanding issues, but it was his misfortune — and everyone else's — that the onset of the economic depression upset the will of the nations to reach agreement.

Meanwhile the government's domestic policies were proving singularly unsuccessful. The legislative programme was crippled either by Liberal opposition in the Commons or by Conservative opposition in the Lords. This would not have damaged the Labour Party if the government had produced a reasonable plan for grappling with the great issue of unemployment, and had either secured its approval by Parliament or resigned. But in fact, nothing effective was even agreed by the Cabinet. Naturally, this exacerbated dissension within the party. The annual conference of 1930 saw a powerful challenge from Mosley, whose Memorandum had been rejected by the Cabinet; and a resolution supporting his policy was only narrowly defeated. Within the parliamentary party there was also trouble, some of it with Mosley and some of it with the I.L.P. Mosley actually founded a New Party, to which he won over four other Labour M.P.s, and this resulted in their expulsion. At the same time, the I.L.P. was seeking to force its M.P.s to obey its own policy decisions rather than those of the Labour Party; and negotiations on this vexed question between the Labour Party National Executive and the leaders of the I.L.P. took place in 1930 and were still dragging on when the government fell in 1931.

The international financial crisis which brought the government down occurred in the summer of 1931. The collapse in May of the Credit Anstalt, a bank in Vienna, led to a loss of confidence and a drain of gold from London, where many foreign banks held short-term investments. In August the government faced the alternatives of abandon-

ing the gold standard or securing fresh loans in Paris and
New York; but the New York bankers would only help if
they were sure that the government was taking sufficient
measures of retrenchment to restore confidence on orthodox
lines. This meant, in fact, cuts in civil service pay and in
the pay of the forces, and also in employment benefits. A
substantial minority of the Cabinet would not accept the
unemployment cuts; but the only alternative seemed to be
a revenue tariff, and this was impracticable as the Liberals
would not have accepted it.

Under the circumstances of the crisis, with a serious
division in the Cabinet, it was decided to consult the
National Executive of the party and also the General
Council of the T.U.C. This was done on 20th August,
when both bodies were summoned to hear statements by
MacDonald and Snowden. After a few questions the meeting broke up, so that the two bodies could consider their
attitude separately; and the General Council sent a small
delegation, including Citrine, the T.U.C. secretary, and
Bevin, the secretary of the big new amalgamation, the
Transport and General Workers Union, to tell Snowden
that they could not agree to the cuts. As Sidney Webb
told his wife: 'The General Council are pigs. They wont
agree to any cuts.'[3] MacDonald began to talk about the
possibility of a Coalition Government, although the members of his Cabinet demurred.

On 23rd August MacDonald resigned office, and early
next morning he accepted the King's commission to form
a new government with the support of the Liberals and
Conservatives. He announced his decision to his aston-
ished Labour colleagues later the same morning. No discussion took place; the ministers who were not joining the
new Cabinet trooped off together, and later that day a
'Council of War', as Dalton calls it in his memoirs, met
in the party secretary's room at Transport House (the new
party and T.U.C. headquarters) to rally the party in
opposition to MacDonald's new government. Those present besides Henderson, the party secretary, were Lansbury,

who had also been in the Cabinet, Citrine and Bevin, Middleton, the assistant secretary of the party, and Francis Hirst, who was chairman of the National Executive and also, incidentally, a member of Bevin's union. 'This is like the General Strike,' said Bevin, 'I'm prepared to put everything in'; and then the group sent for a representative of the *Daily Herald*, whose policy was under the joint control of the party and the T.U.C., in order to 'settle the line of to-morrow's leader'.[4] A new era in the history of the party had begun : the MacDonald era was over ; the control of the party was passing to the extra-parliamentary organs again, and to the T.U.C.

(5)

For nine years MacDonald had dominated the Labour Party, and for nine years he had held an authority which no single individual had ever possessed over its members before. He had received great loyalty from the parliamentary party, and not least from the trade unionists. But the final demands of the 1931 crisis were too great a strain on that loyalty.

The rights and wrongs of the conflict between Mac-Donald and his party have been debated bitterly ever since. Was MacDonald a 'traitor' to his party or was he the 'saviour' of his country ? We can probably allow him at least an honesty of purpose. He knew very little about economics and had to rely upon Snowden, who was a broken reed. He had devoted the previous two years to external affairs and diplomacy and had simply not kept in touch, either with domestic affairs generally or with the rank and file of the labour movement. Consequently, he exaggerated the gravity of the financial crisis and over-estimated his own influence inside the labour movement. He expected to carry about half the parliamentary party with him into his so-called 'National' government; but when his supporters were all counted, they amounted to only Snowden and Thomas, his colleagues in the new government, his son Malcolm, and four others.

The MacDonald Leadership (1922-31)

It has been said that in this crisis the trade-union leaders acted with narrow selfishness, determined to refuse any sort of sacrifice by their members even though the country was in the direst straits. Of course, the trade-union leaders did have sectional interests to serve, but it is noteworthy that the ablest of them — in particular, Bevin and Citrine — understood a great deal more about economics than Mac-Donald and Snowden did, and had an idea of how absurd the whole crisis was. Bevin had been a member of Mac-Donald's Economic Advisory Council and had really paid attention to the discussions, and especially to what was being said by Keynes and G. D. H. Cole. When he disagreed with MacDonald, he knew what he was talking about. But the abstract problems of economic theory were not widely understood at the time. The firmness of the trade-union leadership, and the lack of contact between MacDonald and his parliamentary following, saw to it that when the immediate crisis was over MacDonald was left on one side, in the office of Prime Minister, but virtually without personal supporters; and on the other side was all but a tiny fragment of the Labour Party and the whole trade-union movement, united in bitter opposition, and under a new and very different leadership.

NOTES

1. MacDonald to O. G. Villard, 15 Jan. 1923, quoted by M. S. Venkataramani in *Political Studies*, viii (1960), 237.
2. Alan Bullock, *Life and Times of Ernest Bevin*, i (1960), 204.
3. Diary, 22 Aug. 1931, M. I. Cole (ed.), *Beatrice Webb's Diaries, 1924-1932* (1956), p. 281.
4. Hugh Dalton, *Call Back Yesterday* (1953), p. 274.

FURTHER READING

R. W. Lyman has provided a most judicious study of the 1924 government in his *First Labour Government, 1924* (1957). This may be read in conjunction with a newly-published memorandum on the subject by Sidney Webb, for which see *Political Quarterly*, xxxii (1961). Nothing comparable exists for 1929-31, but there is much valuable material in the strongly pro-MacDonald study by Reginald Bassett,

1931: Political Crisis (1958). A helpful examination of Arthur Henderson as Foreign Secretary, by H. R. Winkler, appears in G. A. Craig and F. Gilbert (ed.), *The Diplomats, 1919–39* (Princeton, N.J., 1953). The following works are useful for the light they throw on events within the labour movement at this time: Alan Bullock, *Life and Times of Ernest Bevin*, i (1960); Fenner Brockway, *Inside the Left* (1942); M. I. Cole (ed.), *Beatrice Webb's Diaries, 1924–1932* (1956). For the Communist Party, see Henry Pelling, *British Communist Party: A Historical Profile* (1958). A useful book on the General Strike, in addition to the biography of Bevin, is Julian Symons, *The General Strike* (1957).

CHAPTER V

Convalescence : The General Council's Party
(1931-40)

(1)

On 25th August 1931 the T.U.C. and the extra-parliamentary party took control of the parliamentary party and disavowed the leadership of MacDonald. The main political crisis was over, so far as the Labour Party was concerned : but its consequences still had to be worked out. The parliamentary party's Consultative Committee, which had been its liaison committee with the Labour Cabinet, held two meetings with the National Executive and the General Council of the T.U.C. before, on 28th August, a full meeting of the parliamentary party took place. And when the parliamentary party did meet, it met at Transport House, with the members of the General Council of the T.U.C. present. According to Dalton, this was 'an innovation, suggested by Uncle [Henderson] to mark unity'.[1] One may suspect, however, that it was an innovation designed to *preserve* unity — by intimidating the waverers. Only one of the four Labour members of MacDonald's new Cabinet attended : this was Lord Sankey, who was heard out respectfully but who won no support. Henderson was elected leader of the parliamentary party by an overwhelming majority.

The influence of the General Council and particularly of Bevin, its dominating personality, on the fortunes of the Labour Party at this juncture has perhaps not been properly appreciated. Bevin had established his claim to rank as a national leader by his effective role in the General Strike. Now aged 50, he was at the height of his powers,

71

and his position inside his own union, the Transport and General Workers, was supreme, for he had by now consolidated the amalgamations of the early 1920's which were also his own work. He had been responsible for building Transport House, which from the date of its completion in 1928 was for a generation not only the headquarters of his union, but also the home of both the T.U.C. and the Labour Party. In 1929, as chairman of the board of the *Daily Herald*, he had made the agreement with Odhams whereby the paper obtained fresh capital and rose to a circulation of well over a million. In theory, the politics of the paper were controlled by the T.U.C. and the Labour Party, but in practice this meant Bevin, as was generally acknowledged. It is true that he was not an M.P.; but his union had sponsored twelve of the existing members of the parliamentary party. He was not on the National Executive; but a member of his union, Hirst, was at the time its chairman, and as such was to be chairman of the forthcoming annual conference of the party. Finally, at the party conference, the Transport and General Workers would have a vote of 235,000, which was almost 10 per cent of the total vote of all the delegates present.

It is true, of course, that Henderson still had great influence. He was still secretary of the party, as he had been for twenty years, and he had been the leader of the Cabinet minority opposed to MacDonald. But Henderson's role in the crisis was not as decisive as Bevin's. As always, Henderson was opposed to a complete break with MacDonald. He had not fully made up his mind to leave the Cabinet on the question of unemployment cuts until he had heard the views of Bevin and Citrine; and he still hoped that there would be no final separation of MacDonald from the party, but rather a temporary divergence like what had happened during the war. Finally, Henderson had only become leader of the parliamentary party with considerable reluctance. He was now 68 and he did not feel that he was ever likely to take office again.

Meanwhile, MacDonald, almost devoid of supporters

CLEMENT ATTLEE (b. 1883)

from the Parliamentary Labour Party, found himself a prisoner of his new allies. In September the new government went off the gold standard without greatly upsetting the City, although the Labour Cabinet had been warned that such an act was quite unthinkable. Later that month the Conservatives began to increase their pressure for a general election. Neville Chamberlain, who was the most vigorous of the Conservative leaders, sought to retain MacDonald while getting rid of the Liberals: this would enable them to win the election and then go for Tariff Reform. But MacDonald did not like the idea. As Sir Clive Wigram, the King's Private Secretary, wrote to the King on 28th September:

> He does not like the idea of smashing up the Labour Party at the head of a Conservative association. He does not know how to run with the hares and hunt with the hounds. He has hopes of sitting tight now and attracting a following of the Labour Party. This may take a long time.[2]

On the same day, however, the National Executive met and formally expelled MacDonald and his colleagues from the Labour Party. It did not look as if there was much prospect of 'attracting a following of the Labour Party'.

Under these circumstances, MacDonald began to think of perpetuating the Coalition by fighting a general election and perhaps thereby building up his little National Labour group. He could not contemplate this without Liberal support; but the Conservatives, who were anxious to introduce Tariff Reform, did not really want to keep the Liberals in the Coalition. Eventually, a compromise was reached; the Liberals stayed in, but agreed to an election in which they would put forward their own slightly different programme. But so far as possible, the fiscal issue would be avoided in the campaign; all National candidates would seek a general mandate, a 'doctor's mandate' as it was called, to deal with the financial crisis. On these terms, a dissolution took place and the general election followed before the end of October.

The election was marked by a bitter campaign against the Labour Party, conducted by all the National candidates but in particular by the Labour Party's own former leaders. Snowden made a truly remarkable election broadcast, in which he spoke of the Labour Party's policy — very little different from what he himself had advocated for years — as 'Bolshevism run mad'. In the majority of contests there was only one National candidate, who obtained the united vote of the Conservative and Liberal parties, together with any Labour vote which had followed MacDonald and Snowden. Thus even if the Labour poll had been as large as in 1929 the party would have lost many of its seats. In fact, the Labour poll dropped from 8 million to 6 million — not such a large fall, considering all that had happened — but its parliamentary position was staggeringly weakened. Only forty-six official party members returned to the new Commons, together with five I.L.P. representatives who had fought the election separately. MacDonald and his little National Labour group numbered thirteen in the new House, but both Mosley's New Party and the Communists failed to win a single seat.

Of the old Labour Government, Lansbury was the only Cabinet minister to survive on the opposition side; and there were only two junior ministers left, Attlee and Sir Stafford Cripps, who had been Solicitor-General. As is usual when the parliamentary party is at the bottom of its fortunes, most of its members were trade unionists, especially miners. In fact, exactly half the party consisted of candidates sponsored by the Miners Federation. The only area of the country which now had any large proportion of Labour M.P.s was South Wales, where about a third of the party had their seats. It was no wonder that the parliamentary party failed to retain the prestige and authority that it had held inside the labour movement in the preceding decade.

(2)

For the first year of the new Parliament Henderson continued as titular leader, but as he was not in the Commons and was in any case spending much time in Geneva as President of the Disarmament Conference, Lansbury served as acting leader with Attlee as his deputy. In the autumn of 1932 Henderson resigned the leadership, though he remained secretary of the extra-parliamentary party; and Lansbury now became titular as well as actual leader in the House. But obviously the parliamentary party was a poor and nerveless thing in this Parliament of the early 1930's. Lansbury himself was already 72, and was in any case a poor leader because of his tendency towards a woolly-minded sentimentality. His two ablest assistants, Attlee and Cripps, both seemed to be suffering from the shock of the electoral defeat, and inclined to advocate policies of extreme and barren militancy. Cripps, for instance, made speeches about the 'sinister influence' of Buckingham Palace and the need for a temporary dictatorship by the party if Labour should win a general election. Attlee was more discreet in his utterances, but his views were almost as extreme. These two men were both public school men (Attlee had been at Haileybury, Cripps at Winchester) and it took time for them to establish relations of trust, either with their other parliamentary colleagues on the one hand, or with the extra-parliamentary movement on the other. At first Lansbury was the only member of the parliamentary party to sit on the National Executive, which he did by virtue of his position as parliamentary leader; and the liaison with the bulk of the trade-union world — except the Miners Federation — was also poor.

Under these conditions, it might be supposed that the I.L.P. would find its way back into the Labour Party. What the I.L.P. leaders had originally objected to, after all, was the conservatism of the Labour Party's programme and policy in the days of MacDonald. But this had turned into an assertion of the I.L.P.'s right to determine its M.P.s' voting behaviour as a separate group in the House of Commons. When this was denied, its candidates fought the 1931 election as a separate group, and in 1932 by conference decision the I.L.P. disaffiliated from the Labour Party. Thus was ended an association which had been continuous from the foundation of the Labour Party, and which had indeed been largely responsible for the Labour Party's successful establishment. But things had changed radically in the 1920's. The I.L.P. had become an extremist group, largely centred upon Clydeside; and the effect of disaffiliation, while damaging to the Labour Party, was catastrophic to the I.L.P. Many of its older members at once resigned, and others soon came to realise that it had no future as an electoral rival to the Labour Party. From almost 17,000 members in 1932 the total steadily declined to a mere 4400 in 1935.

With the loss of the I.L.P., it was natural that attempts should be made to found a new Socialist society within the Labour Party, for those who wished to devise and propagate an advanced Socialist programme. Two small groups had already come into existence : one of them was the New Fabian Research Bureau, which was intended to revitalise the long moribund Fabian Society; the other was the Society for Socialist Inquiry and Propaganda, which was really for the dissemination of the research undertaken by the other body. The N.F.R.B. continued its work and finally in 1939 was reunited with the Fabian Society, giving the older body new energy and receiving in return the remaining assets of the Society. But the S.S.I.P. was amalgamated with a group which left the I.L.P. when it disaffiliated from the Labour Party, and was reconstituted as the Socialist League, with E. F. Wise, from the I.L.P., as its first chairman. Wise died suddenly in 1933, and soon it was being run by Stafford Cripps. Unlike the N.F.R.B., it soon began to run into conflict with the policy of the party and looked as if it would repeat the later history of the I.L.P.

In this period of disorder among the more committed

Socialists and intellectuals, the General Council of the T.U.C. under the leadership of Bevin and Citrine abandoned its usual role of being the sheet-anchor of the party and instead moved in to take the helm. Citrine demanded that 'the General Council should be regarded as having an integral right to initiate and participate in any political matter which it deems to be of direct concern to its constituents'.[3] For this purpose the National Joint Council, which had originally been established in 1921, was reconstituted on a new basis. Instead of the General Council, the parliamentary party, and the National Executive having equal representation on it, it was remodelled so that the General Council alone had a majority of its members. Henceforward it was to meet at least once a month, and also was to be summoned in any emergency requiring prompt action. Although its purpose was theoretically only consultative, in fact its decisions were bound to carry great authority inside the movement, and it would have been highly embarrassing for the parliamentary party or any other body inside the party to have gone counter to it on any major issue.

The records show that the National Council of Labour was constantly meeting in the 1930's and constantly issuing statements on policy, and Bevin himself, who served on it from 1931 to 1937, regarded these decisions as binding even upon the parliamentary leader. In 1933, for instance, he wrote to Lansbury to protest against his speaking on the platform of the Socialist League without getting prior permission from the National Council of Labour. On this occasion Lansbury dug in his rather weary toes. 'I do not think', he replied, 'that I am called upon to ask permission from anybody to do this — and certainly have no intention of doing so.'[4] At the same time, he made no attempt to assert his own authority as parliamentary leader. At the 1934 party conference, he even admitted that he did not regard himself as the 'leader', but rather as no more than the 'spokesman', of the party.[5]

With the expansion of Japan in the Far East and the

rise to power of Hitler in Germany in 1933, foreign policy began to assume a new urgency, and it was in this sphere that the most serious divergencies began to appear between the parliamentary 'spokesman' and the National Council of Labour. Lansbury was a pacifist with Marxian under-tones: he was not only opposed to the use of armaments for self-defence, but to the very existence of the League of Nations, which he regarded as a society of rich powers banded against the 'have-nots'. The union leaders, on the other hand, took a more practical view of foreign affairs based upon their industrial experience, and regarded collective security through the League as the equivalent of collective bargaining through a trade union. Although Henderson had great hopes of disarmament, this was also in reality his view. But he was now too old and infirm to be of much assistance. He had been re-elected to Parliament in 1933, but in 1934 he resigned the secretaryship of the party and in 1935 he died.

Henderson's resignation from the secretaryship opened up the whole question of the future control of the political side of the movement; for although in the previous three years he had largely ceased to exercise control as he had done in the past, particularly during and just after the war, it was clear that a younger man might reassert power in this office. After the party's misfortunes with MacDonald, however, there was a strong tendency to mistrust any concentration of power in the hands of one man. It was therefore decided that Henderson's successor should not be allowed to become a Member of Parliament. This ruled out Herbert Morrison, probably the most powerful contender, who had built up the London Labour Party to such a degree of strength that in this same year it was able to win control of the London County Council — a control which it has never since lost. But it also ruled out other possible contenders with parliamentary ambitions. In the upshot, the choice fell upon Jimmy Middleton, the quiet-spoken official who had been assistant secretary ever since 1903. After this, it was many years before the post of secretary again assumed major importance : but the National Executive to some extent gained in collective weight.

After this, then, there was a rough division of policy-making functions between the National Council of Labour (dominated by Bevin and Citrine) and the National Executive (dominated by politicians, but elected by the union block vote at annual conferences). The National Council determined the outlines of policy, declaring for collective security, opposition to Fascism, refusal to collaborate with the Communists in a new 'United Front', and so on. The National Executive had a powerful Policy Sub-Committee, consisting of Attlee and Cripps, who were now on the National Executive, and the other leading younger contenders for parliamentary honours, several of them still being outside Parliament : Herbert Morrison, Hugh Dalton, Arthur Greenwood. The Sub-Committee was very active in drawing up detailed legislative and administrative programmes for a Labour Government, within the general policies laid down by the Council of Labour. The concept of 'planning' was only now being evolved, and the Labour Party's economic experts were just awakening to the need to prepare every step of their proposed transition to Socialism, in such a way that the economy would continue to function satisfactorily throughout. In this process of reshaping policy, the Roosevelt New Deal, the Russian Five-Year Plan, and even the work of Schacht in Nazi Germany, all had their impact.

In 1935 it seemed that a new general election was imminent; and while the results of the election would, it was hoped, provide an opportunity for the improvement of the parliamentary leadership, it was the parliamentary leadership which had to conduct the election campaign. The dilemma was a real one, for the party could not rely upon Lansbury to provide a skilful management of the election, or even to follow party policy in his own utterances. It has already been pointed out that his attitude on foreign policy was in conflict with that of the party; and with Mussolini's impending attack upon Abyssinia, foreign affairs had assumed the highest importance. The 'Peace Ballot', conducted in the course of the summer by members of the League of Nations Union, showed that there was in fact a remarkably strong sentiment in the country in favour of 'sanctions' by the League, if necessary involving the use of force. To continue to have a pacifist as leader of the party would only lead to misunderstandings: yet Lansbury resisted all hints that it was time for him to resign. The issue came to a head at the 1935 annual conference of the party, when Lansbury opposed a resolution reaffirming the policy laid down by the National Council of Labour. Ernest Bevin, speaking immediately after Lansbury, accused him directly of 'hawking your conscience around from body to body asking to be told what you ought to do with it'. The resolution was carried by an overwhelming majority, and Lansbury thereupon resigned. He was replaced by Attlee on a temporary basis for the remainder of the parliamentary session; and so Attlee acted as leader during the general election which took place in November. For the first time the Labour Party's chief spokesman was not a man of working-class origin.

The election was fought by the National Government very largely on the issue of foreign policy, and on the question of collective security Baldwin, who was now Prime Minister in place of MacDonald, very largely stole the Labour Party's thunder. The result was that although the Labour Party made a considerable recovery, it still did not get back even to its 1929 strength. Its total poll was over 8 million again, but the Conservatives alone got almost 10½ million. The Labour Party did well once more in the London area and recovered much lost ground in Yorkshire and Scotland. The total number of seats won was 154, of which 79 were won by trade-union-sponsored candidates: a majority but only a small majority this time. Many of the abler members of the 1929 Parliament now reappeared — Morrison, Dalton, and Emanuel Shinwell included. The National Labour group led by MacDonald sank to eight, MacDonald himself being defeated by Shinwell; and one

Communist, Willie Gallacher, was elected. The I.L.P. retained four seats, all in Glasgow, but was obviously a waning force. It could safely be asserted that the electorate showed little sympathy for splinter groups on the Left or for that matter on the Right.

(3)

The first issue to face the new parliamentary party was that of its own leadership. Clynes had been re-elected to the Commons, but he was now 66 and so could hardly expect a long term in the office. He refused to stand. This left three main contenders — Attlee, the incumbent, described by the *New Statesman* as 'a natural Adjutant, but not a General'; Arthur Greenwood, a former economics lecturer who had been Minister of Health in the 1929 government; and Herbert Morrison, once a Cockney errand-boy but also a former minister. Morrison was supported by Dalton and also had the backing of many London members; Greenwood was supported by Bevin, who had clashed with Morrison, and probably by the newly-elected trade unionists generally; Attlee was backed by the re-elected M.P.s who had grown to like him in the previous Parliament. On a first vote, Attlee got 58 votes, Morrison 44, and Greenwood 33; on a second vote Attlee secured almost all Greenwood's votes, partly because he was still thought to be only a temporary leader. But he grew in authority and gradually consolidated his position, profiting by the rivalries of the other potential candidates, and gradually winning the respect of Bevin and other union leaders outside the House.

For a time, however, there was still a distinct contrast between the National Council of Labour's policy of collective security and the actual attitude of the parliamentary party, which continued to oppose the defence estimates. The parliamentary party always contained a number of out-and-out pacifists, and anti-militarist feeling remained strong in its ranks: this had an effect on the party's decisions as to particular issues in the House. But in 1936

Dalton, who was keen on rearmament, was chairman of the National Executive, and Bevin was simultaneously chairman of the General Council. Between them they contrived to swing the policy of the parliamentary party, being assisted in this by the outbreak of the Spanish Civil War. Their method of action was as follows: a strong statement was made by the National Council of Labour in the summer; this was then endorsed by the Trades Union Congress which as usual met early in September. The Labour Party Conference followed a month later in October — a practice initiated in 1924 when it had been postponed from June owing to the difficulty of Members of Parliament attending before the House had risen. It was difficult, therefore, for Conference not to follow the strong lead given by the National Council of Labour and by Congress — as Herbert Morrison found on this particular occasion, which committed the movement to the support of the existing rearmament programme. Morrison was resisting throughout the summer but when the conference met in October he did not speak, and the resolution was easily carried.

The Spanish Civil War aroused public opinion within the labour movement to a degree that no foreign war had ever done before, unless we go back to the American Civil War. There was widespread enthusiasm for the Spanish Republicans, as against the army clique led by General Franco, and although at first the National Council of Labour advocated non-intervention, this policy was soon abandoned as it was seen to be ineffective. The Communist Party, now rapidly growing in strength since the abandonment of its sectarian policy in 1933, acted as recruiting agent for the International Brigade, which had been established on the orders of the Communist International. Many young men, not only Communist Party members or sympathisers, went off to join the Brigade or to work behind the lines, and a considerable impetus was given to the policy of the 'United Front' of all parties on the Left against the threat of Fascism. The mood of the times was exemplified by the sensational success of the Left Book Club, founded by Victor Gollancz to advocate this cause.

The growth of Socialist sympathies in all sections of the population since 1931 had by no means failed to benefit the Labour Party itself. The individual membership of the party had doubled in the years 1928 to 1937, and the only trouble was that the Socialist League, which had replaced the I.L.P. as an affiliated Socialist society, was showing much the same hostility to general conference decisions as its predecessor had done. The Socialist League wished to form a 'United Front' with the Communists and the I.L.P., but this was resisted by the National Council of Labour, as the union officials and the more senior Labour Party leaders had a vivid recollection of the trouble that they had had from the Communists in earlier years. Besides, as they realised, the Communists would have been a heavy liability for the Labour Party at election time.

In order to provide an alternative outlet for the feelings of the individual members of the party, and so to overcome the tendency that many of them had to side with bodies like the I.L.P. or Socialist League, Dalton advocated the policy of allowing the constituency parties to elect their own members to the National Executive. This was a concession which the unions were unwilling to make, but Dalton persuaded Bevin to agree and it was introduced at the 1937 conference. The number of seats made available to the constituency parties was simultaneously increased from five to seven. It was also decided to move the conference date to Whitsuntide to avoid immediately following the T.U.C. The new Executive election system came into force at once, and one or two representatives of the intellectual Left at once appeared on the National Executive, in particular Harold Laski and D. N. Pritt. But only one or two : as Dalton had foreseen, these representatives were largely the prisoners of the National Executive majority; and the conference then proceeded to disaffiliate the Socialist League and to reject the policy of the 'United Front'. Cripps knew that he had been beaten and he decided upon a voluntary dissolution of the Socialist League.

The final effort of Cripps and others to collaborate with the Communists and the I.L.P. came in 1939. By this time the effort was somewhat quixotic, for the Communist Party had been not a little discredited by the behaviour of the Communists in Spain in attacking their Anarchist comrades-in-arms, and also by Stalin's purges of the Russian army and Comintern hierarchy. Nevertheless, Cripps, who was himself a wealthy man as a result of his success at the bar, decided to conduct a nation-wide campaign for what was now called the 'Popular Front'. This led to his expulsion from the Labour Party by the National Executive, with only two dissentients (Ellen Wilkinson and Pritt, but not Laski). His principal followers, Charles Trevelyan, Aneurin Bevan, and George Strauss, were also expelled. This action was endorsed by an overwhelming majority by the party conference.

By this time the danger of war had become acute. At the time of Munich the National Council of Labour had spoken out against concessions to Hitler; and Churchill is said to have telephoned Attlee on 20th September 1938 to tell him 'Your declaration does honour to the British nation'.[6] On several occasions, deputations of the three executives of the Labour movement — the parliamentary party, the National Executive and the General Council — called upon Chamberlain or Halifax, his Foreign Minister, to discuss the situation and to demand a change of policy. This only came in March, when the occupation of Prague by the Germans finally convinced the government that Hitler was quite untrustworthy.

Almost immediately afterwards, the government decided to introduce conscription. Although the Labour Party had accepted the need for rearmament since 1937 — which was not too bad a record for an opposition party interested in social reform and provided with very little information on defence questions by the government — it seemed to show considerable weakness in maintaining its hostility to conscription. Continuing suspicion of Chamberlain's intentions had a good deal to do with this. As soon as the measure was passed, the labour movement accepted it quite loyally; and Attlee has subsequently admitted that he thinks the attempt to prevent it was a mistake.[7] At the time, Dalton and a few others refused to vote against it in the House — exercising the conscience clause for a very different purpose from that for which it had been introduced.

(4)

On 1st September Hitler invaded Poland and two days later Britain declared war. In the mounting crisis immediately preceding the declaration, the National Council of Labour had been meeting, and a committee consisting of Dalton, Morrison, and Citrine had been appointed to confer with the Prime Minister (Attlee being ill at the time). On 2nd September a joint meeting of the National Executive and of the Executive of the parliamentary party decided that the party should not join the government. The General Council of the T.U.C. had no part in this decision because the T.U.C. was just then taking place at Bridlington. But there was no possibility of disagreement on the issue. Shortly afterwards, an electoral truce was agreed upon as in 1914.

Although Chamberlain secured the co-operation of Churchill and other Conservative dissentients in reconstructing his government, the hostility between the National Government and the Labour Opposition remained strong. Moreover, there seemed to be plenty to criticise in the conduct of the war. A distinct air of complacency was noticeable in Whitehall during what became known as 'the phoney war'. It was only in April 1940, just after Chamberlain had made a speech saying that Hitler 'had missed the bus', that the atmosphere suddenly changed, as a result of the German attack on Scandinavia. Set-backs to Allied arms in this area were deeply galling, for they implied an inferiority in naval warfare as well as in purely military operations. A new Conservative 'cave' formed in opposition to Chamberlain, and in the great debate of early May the Labour Party decided to press a vote of censure. Chamberlain accepted the challenge defiantly but his majority sank to only eighty votes.

The invasion of the Low Countries and France was now taking place. The demands for a coalition were insistent, and Chamberlain asked Attlee whether the Labour Party would join the government, either under himself or under some other leader. Attlee referred the question to the National Executive, which was then attending the party conference at Bournemouth. The reply was that the party would take office only under another leader. This determined Chamberlain's fate and he resigned forthwith. A consultation then took place between Chamberlain, Halifax, and Churchill. It was agreed that Halifax was hardly suitable as Prime Minister owing to being in the Lords; and the post then fell to Churchill. Attlee discussed the new ministry with Churchill and agreed to a suggested allocation of the major offices. He then returned to Bournemouth to secure the party's confirmation of what he had done.

Attlee gave an account of his actions to meetings of the National Executive and the General Council of the T.U.C. After each had agreed unanimously with what he had done, an emergency resolution in this sense was moved at the following session of Conference. It was carried by an overwhelming vote. Thus Labour's acceptance of office was done in the most formal fashion, following procedure that was drawn up after the 1931 crisis, and taking advantage of the fact that Conference was in session. A new phase of the party's history was about to begin.

NOTES

1. Dalton, *Call Back Yesterday*, p. 277.
2. Harold Nicolson, *King George V* (1952), p. 491.
3. Report of meeting in T.U.C. file, quoted V. L. Allen, *Trade Unions and the Government* (1960), p. 258.

4. Lansbury to Bevin, March 1933, quoted Raymond Postgate, *Life of George Lansbury* (1951), p. 288.
5. *Labour Party Annual Report*, 1934, p. 146.
6. Hugh Dalton, *The Fateful Years* (1957), p. 185.
7. C. R. Attlee, *As It Happened* (1954), p. 103.

FURTHER READING

Apart from G. D. H. Cole's *History of the Labour Party from 1914*, there is no narrative of the party's history in this period. Most of the biographies mentioned for the preceding period are also of importance for the 1930's, notably Alan Bullock's *Life and Times of Ernest Bevin*, and Fenner Brockway's memoirs, *Inside the Left*. To these should be added Raymond Postgate's *Life of George Lansbury* and the second volume of Hugh Dalton's memoirs, *The Fateful Years*. Attlee's first volume of memoirs, *As It Happened*, are of value only to those who can read between the lines. His second volume, *A Prime Minister Remembers*, is somewhat more revealing.

CHAPTER VI

Office and Power under Attlee and Bevin
(1940-50)

(1)

THE period of the 1940's includes both the full five years
of the war-time Coalition and the only slightly shorter
length of the 1945 Parliament, which provided for the first
time a Labour Government with a Commons majority.
Like the earlier periods which we have considered, this one
has a certain unity about it, in spite of the great changes
effected by the end of the war and by the general election.
So far as the Labour Party was concerned, its parliamentary
leaders were in office throughout, and gained power within
the movement as a result. The extra-parliamentary party
and the trade-union movement were consequently under
constant restraint, sometimes critical of government policy
but always anxious to avoid the embarrassment that would
follow if they carried their protests beyond the limits of
friendly admonishment.

The period thus formed a very marked contrast with
the 1930's, when control of the movement was largely in
the hands of the National Council of Labour, on which the
General Council of the T.U.C. had a majority of seats. In
1940 the most powerful personality of the trade-union
movement, Ernest Bevin, was brought in by Churchill to
take office in the government; and the mutual under-
standing and affection that developed between him and
Attlee provided the party with a stronger and more stable
leadership than it had ever had before, even during the
1920's. Not that Attlee could establish the personal position
that MacDonald had had, or could efface the memory of

(*a*) The Dockers' Leader (1920)

(*b*) Minister of Labour (1940)

ERNEST BEVIN (1881–1951)

MacDonald within the party; but he and his colleagues knew that the only possible successor, if he gave up the leadership, was Bevin, and so long as he had Bevin's support he could ignore the occasional intrigues designed to force his resignation as leader, such as that voiced by Laski in 1945, or that in which Cripps took part in 1947. Instead, the degree of collaboration between Attlee and Bevin was remarkable for two men so different in their social origins and experience. As if to symbolise its loss of power, the National Council of Labour suffered a change of its constitution in 1941, whereby the Co-operative Union was brought in on an equal basis of representation with the T.U.C. and the Labour Party. Henceforward it was too clumsy an institution to have any real authority.

(2)

In proportion to its parliamentary strength in 1940, the Labour Party did very well indeed in the apportionment of offices made by Churchill as he became Prime Minister. There was to be a War Cabinet of five members, of whom two were to be Labour men — Attlee and Greenwood. In addition, Ernest Bevin became Minister of Labour and National Service, Herbert Morrison took the post of Minister of Supply, A. V. Alexander became First Lord of the Admiralty as in 1929, Hugh Dalton was Minister of Economic Warfare, and Sir William Jowitt was Solicitor-General. This large share of offices was partly the result of the party's role in the formation of the ministry and partly a recognition that at this time the Labour Party had a larger support in the country than it had in Parliament.

When Labour entered the government, some fresh arrangements had to be made for running the parliamentary party. The Parliamentary Executive therefore recommended, and the parliamentary party agreed to, the appointment of an Administrative Committee, consisting of members who were not ministers. While Attlee was to remain leader of the party, and with other ministers was to have access to meetings of the Administrative Committee, it was not expected that his attendance or that of other ministers would be very frequent. It was also agreed that the office of Leader of the Opposition should lapse for the duration of the Coalition. This meant that the salary of £2000 paid by the state to the Leader of the Opposition under the Ministers of the Crown Act, 1937, went into abeyance. Instead, H. B. Lees Smith, a senior Labour M.P. who had not been offered a post in the government, was chosen as Acting Chairman of the Parliamentary Party and hence became unofficial Leader of the Opposition. This arrangement was somewhat vexing to another prominent Labour member who had not taken office, Emanuel Shinwell. Shinwell had refused an appointment offered him by Churchill because he thought it unsuitable; and he would have been a somewhat more effective Opposition leader than Lees Smith — in fact, rather too effective for the liking of the party as a whole.

As the war went on, changes took place in the government, but the rough balance of the parties was preserved. In September 1940 the War Cabinet was enlarged, and Bevin was brought in to make up a Labour group of three in a total of seven members. In October, Morrison was moved from Supply to the much more suitable post of Home Secretary and Minister of Home Security, where his knowledge of London government and personal popularity helped him much. In February 1941 Thomas Johnston became Secretary of State for Scotland. Then in February 1942 a more considerable reshuffle of government posts was made. Greenwood, who had not been a great success as a minister, relinquished office altogether; but Cripps, who had been sent by Churchill as ambassador to Moscow, and who had come back with a somewhat unreal reputation as the man responsible for the improvement in Anglo-Soviet relations since the invasion of Russia, now entered the War Cabinet as Lord Privy Seal and Leader of the House of Commons — an extraordinary advance for one who had been ignominiously expelled from the Labour

Party for political extremism in 1939. Dalton moved to the Board of Trade and Attlee, while acknowledged now as Deputy Premier, also took the Dominions Office.

Cripps did not prove an entire success in his high office, and particularly as Leader of the House. Towards the end of the year, therefore, Churchill decided to move him to an administrative office outside the War Cabinet — that of Minister of Aircraft Production, admittedly a key post, and one in which his scientific training was of value. To restore the political balance, Morrison was brought into the War Cabinet, while retaining his post as Home Secretary and Minister of Home Security. Little further adjustment of responsibilities affecting the principal Labour ministers was made before 1945. The team was now working together well and the change in the fortunes of British arms removed one obvious incentive for change in the ministry.

The Coalition Government on the whole worked far more smoothly than that of the First World War. The very extremity of the crisis in 1940 made the Service chiefs more amenable to a single political control; the high reputation of Churchill as a strategist owed not a little to his length of experience and to the recognition that he almost alone had seen the need for urgent rearmament in the 1930's; and the readiness with which he could invigorate public opinion through B.B.C. broadcasts gave him a popular support which Lloyd George a quarter of a century earlier could only obtain by the grace of the press barons. At the same time, Churchill accepted the need for effective compromise between the political parties in the working out of domestic policy — a subject which really did not interest him very much while the war continued.

Much of the administration of home affairs during the war was conducted by Attlee. As the Prime Minister's deputy, he presided over Cabinets when Churchill was abroad; and as the need for high-level consultations with Allied leaders led Churchill to travel more frequently, Attlee's chairmanship became more and more practised. By contrast with Churchill's, Attlee's Cabinets disposed rapidly of the business that faced them : decisions were reached quickly instead of being postponed. All this not only widened Attlee's experience; it heightened his stature with his own colleagues, especially with Bevin, who had had little contact with him before 1940. The Labour ministers were also able to secure the passage of a limited amount of social legislation in the later part of the war. Prominent in this sphere were Thomas Johnston's hydro-electric scheme for the Scottish Highlands, Ernest Bevin's Catering Wages Act, and Dalton's Location of Industry Act, though the final stages of the latter were passed only after the end of the Coalition. It is true that little or no action was taken to implement a number of major commissions of enquiry which recommended reforms : this was notably the case with the Beveridge Report on Social Insurance, published in 1942 and taken up with much enthusiasm by the Press, but never officially approved of by the Coalition Government. Nevertheless, one very important change in the sphere of financial policy was accepted in 1944, when the principle of the need to secure full employment by government action was acknowledged in a White Paper. Attlee used this in a letter to Laski as a justification for the Labour Party's membership of the Coalition Government. 'The acceptance of these assumptions', he wrote, 'has its effect both in legislation and in administration, but its gradualness tends to hide our appreciation of the facts'.[1]

A subtle change came over the Coalition, however, as victory became imminent. Attlee tells us in his memoirs :

> I found . . . that it was more and more difficult to get post-war projects before the Cabinet. Agreements arrived at after long discussion by a Committee, on which both parties were fully represented, were blocked by the opposition of certain members of the Government who evinced a quite new interest in subjects hitherto outside the range of their attention.[2]

The ending of the war with Germany in May 1945 was of course the decisive turning-point. Thereafter, it was only a matter of jockeying for position by the two parties. Churchill, reckoning that his own great reputation would be of most value to the Conservatives immediately after the achievement of victory, suggested one of two alternatives to the Labour Party — either an immediate election or a continuation of the Coalition until the defeat of Japan. As the Labour Party Conference was meeting over Whitsun, Attlee was able to consult the National Executive as well as his immediate colleagues in the government in framing his reply. He suggested instead that the Coalition should continue until the autumn, which would give more time for the organisation of the campaign and the preparation of the list of voters.

Churchill, however, decided to yield to the pressure of his Conservative Party campaign advisers to hold the election as soon as practicable. Accordingly, the Labour Ministers handed in their seals of office later in May and the general election took place in July.

(3)

The general election of 1945 was on the whole a quiet one, conducted on an out-of-date register, albeit with a postal vote for the forces. The liveliest issue was that injected by Churchill, to the effect that if the Labour Party won the election, Attlee as Prime Minister would be under the control of Harold Laski, at that time Chairman of the National Executive. Some substance had been given to this possibility by Laski's own declaration that the Labour Party would not be bound by any commitments entered into by Attlee when, as the Leader of the Labour Party, he accompanied Churchill to the Potsdam Conference with Stalin and Truman in June. In a correspondence of increasing asperity, Churchill elaborated his charges on this score, while Attlee rebutted them, saying that 'at no time and in no circumstances has the National Executive Committee ever sought to give, or given, instructions to the Parliamentary Labour Party', and 'The Chairman has not the power to give me instructions'.

93

Naturally, nobody on the Labour Party side was disposed to challenge Attlee's arguments, and when it came to interpreting the Labour Party constitution Churchill was at a disadvantage. Consequently, Attlee got the better of these exchanges. All the same, Churchill was not unjustified in having doubts about the theoretical independence of a Labour Prime Minister, for, as we have seen, some efforts had been made in the 1930's to prevent the emergence of a new leader with as much power as Ramsay MacDonald had had, and the 1933 Conference had laid down a procedure for the Leader to follow in deciding whether to form a government, and how to choose his colleagues. But the matter was too little understood by the electorate to remove the impression that it was simply an election scare on the part of Churchill and his campaign advisers.

The election resulted in a dramatic victory for the Labour Party. Altogether 393 Labour M.P.s were returned, giving them a clear majority of 146 over all other parties. It could not be said, however, that Labour had a clear majority among the voters: the Liberals still held the balance there, but on this occasion the bias present in the constituency system worked in favour of the Labour Party. It is doubtful if the party owed its success to its programme of reform, although this programme, comprising the nationalisation of several industries and promises of major social legislation, was very ably formulated by Herbert Morrison in the manifesto *Let Us Face the Future*. Rather than absorb these details, the electorate was probably voting as usual on the record of the past: the Conservatives had to take the blame for the Munich Agreement, and for the failure to rearm as well as for pre-war unemployment. There was also a good deal of concern lest the post-war situation should resemble that after the First World War, when the lavish promises of Lloyd George had led to very little fulfilment.

A striking feature of the results was that the trade-union-sponsored members of the new Parliamentary Labour Party were now less than a third of the total. The great change since the 1935 election was the flood of youngish middle-class Labour M.P.s, many of them professional men — lawyers, journalists, teachers, doctors, and dons. About two-thirds of the party had never been in Parliament before. This was in fact a new party, one that represented more fully than ever before all classes, all occupations, and all adult age-groups. The contrast with that first, highly homogeneous working-class party of 1906 was especially marked. Yet the natural internal discipline of the party was now immeasurably greater: so great in fact that it proved possible in June 1946 to suspend altogether the Standing Orders forbidding M.P.s to vote against party decisions.

When it came to forming a government, Attlee paid no attention to the procedure laid down by the 1933 Conference. As he later blandly put it in his memoirs, 'the passage of time and further experience has led to these proposals being tacitly dropped'.[3] In point of fact, however, there was a move by Herbert Morrison and others to delay Attlee's acceptance of the King's invitation to form a government until the parliamentary party had met and formally chosen its leader. Morrison claims in his own memoirs that he made this move solely in order to conform with the correct procedure, as formulated by Conference in the 1930's; and this is no doubt true.[4] In the event, however, he did not get his way, as both Attlee and Bevin were anxious to get on with the Cabinet-making. In any case, delay would only have appeared to confirm the truth of Churchill's charges made during the election.

Attlee decided to abandon the war-time system of having a small inner Cabinet. He sought instead a judiciously blended Cabinet of ministers without departments, available for the main Cabinet committee work, and ministers in charge of the main departments. The total came to nineteen. But there was a small group within the nineteen who had the responsibility of supervising whole fields of policy. These were Bevin, the Foreign Minister, who was concerned with all external matters including colonial policy; Herbert Morrison, the Lord President, who had to supervise the legislative programme and determine the order of nationalisation; Arthur Greenwood, the Lord Privy Seal, who in the early part of the war had instructed Beveridge to draw up his famous report, and who was now in charge of the social services; and Hugh Dalton, the Chancellor of the Exchequer, whose office naturally entailed great influence.

Within this inner ring, Attlee retained personal authority of no mean order. Bevin was his closest confidant: yet in making his Cabinet he exchanged the proposed offices of Bevin and Dalton, at first disappointing both men; and Morrison, although claiming that this change was made at his own suggestion, admits that he himself had little intimacy with Attlee: 'It was quite impossible to approach near enough . . . to know what he was really thinking.'[5] Nor can Greenwood have been any more in Attlee's confidence: at any rate, Attlee had no hesitation in dismissing him from office in 1947 on the grounds that, at the age of 68, he was too old. This would not have been so bad for Greenwood if Attlee had not replaced him with Lord Addison, who was ten years older. In the sphere of defence, Attlee at first followed Churchill's example by himself acting as the Minister of Defence, but in 1946 he appointed A. V. Alexander to this office, at the same time excluding the heads of the three services from membership of the Cabinet.

The legislative programme of nationalisation went through Parliament with remarkable smoothness. First of all came the measure nationalising the Bank of England, which met with little opposition from the Conservatives, Churchill himself saying that it 'does not, in my opinion, raise any matter of principle'.[6] Then came the establishment of the National Coal Board, a public but semi-independent body, having a limited responsibility to the Minister of Fuel and Power. Here again there was little spirited opposition to the take-over of what was clearly a very inefficient industry. Rather more controversy was aroused, however, by the establishment of the British Transport Commission in 1947, not so much because it took over the railways and canals, which had already been very unprofitable, as because it also included the road haulage business. It was as a result of this legislation that British Road Services came into existence. The nationalisation of cable and wireless companies and the establishment of public corporations to run the airlines merely continued a policy accepted by earlier governments. In 1948 and 1949 respectively the British Electricity Authority and the Gas Council were set up to take over management of two further public utilities, both of which were already under substantial public control.

The most vigorous political controversy in respect of nationalisation took place over the iron and steel industry. This was deliberately left to the last by the government because of the difficulties of defining how far the nationalisation should go and what the new form of the industry should be. Iron and steel is a very complex industry in which ownership overlaps substantially into engineering and other industries. Furthermore, at the time it was both profitable and comparatively efficient. These considerations led to the Prime Minister secretly sponsoring an enquiry, carried out by Herbert Morrison, into the possibility of the industry accepting a Board of Control appointed by the government, in return for the abandonment of nationalisation. Morrison was able to report a wide measure of agreement for the proposal, but it was hotly opposed in Cabinet by Bevan and others, and was therefore abandoned.[7] To allow further time for the preparation of the measure, an act was passed reducing the delaying power of the House of Lords from two years to one. In 1949 an act was passed to enable the government to purchase the assets of the iron and steel companies, without completely altering the industry's structure. The Lords in fact agreed to this act after persuading the government to postpone the date of its operation until after the forthcoming general election.

Thus the Labour Party's 1945 proposals for nationalisation were all carried out, so far as legislation was concerned, before the end of the Parliament. If they all came into operation, some 20 per cent of the economy, it was estimated, would be in public ownership. Yet, as so often happens, the changes of the period which had the greatest impact on everyday social life were budgetary rather than purely legislative. And in this sphere the government faced the problem not only of redistributing the nation's wealth but also of increasing it so that Britain could pay her way in the world's markets. After the sudden end of American Lend-Lease in 1945, a large dollar loan was negotiated, but the money was spent unexpectedly quickly and a major foreign exchange crisis occurred in 1947. Dalton, the Chancellor, was blamed for not foreseeing this, and in the crisis Stafford Cripps was made Minister for Economic Affairs. Dalton prepared an autumn budget but an indiscretion to a journalist deprived him of office and enabled Cripps to combine the two posts.

Cripps now exercised a wide control over the economic affairs of the nation, and became the most influential person in the government after Attlee and Bevin. He imposed a programme of 'austerity' — heavy taxation on internal consumption and the restriction of overseas purchases and foreign travel, so as to enable the deficit in the country's foreign exchange account to be made up. The unions were persuaded to accept a policy of 'wage restraint' so as to keep down costs and enable British exports to compete effectively abroad. They agreed to this the more willingly because Cripps retained the highly redistributive taxation system which had operated during the war and kept a strict control on the price level.

So far as general popularity was concerned, the most acceptable measures of the Labour Government were in the sphere of the social services. The school leaving age was raised to fifteen, and state scholarships to the universities were increased. The Beveridge social insurance proposals were implemented by the enactment of James Griffiths' National Insurance Act, and Aneurin Bevan as Minister of Health introduced the National Health Service, which provided free medical treatment and free drugs, and which involved the nationalisation of the hospitals. Bevan was less successful in dealing with housing, however, for although he encouraged construction by local authorities for cheap letting, and kept a tight rein on private building, he did not achieve the target of two hundred thousand houses annually which the government had promised.

By far the most contentious areas of policy within the Labour Party itself were foreign affairs and defence. Bevin, as Foreign Secretary, soon found that he was faced by an unexpectedly intransigent attitude on the part of the Russian Government. Realising the economic weakness not only of Britain but also of the rest of Europe, Bevin therefore worked for effective collaboration with the United States. He did much to bring the 'Marshall Plan' into existence, which had a powerfully invigorating effect in stimulating recovery throughout Western Europe; and he was a prime mover in creating the North Atlantic Treaty Organisation. This policy of association with the United States and of re-armament to resist Russian pressure did not commend itself very warmly to the rank and file of the Labour Party. The concept of a 'Socialist' foreign policy, it was felt, had been abandoned: at the very least, an attempt should have been made to retain a position of independence between the capitalist and the Communist world — if possible, to form a bridge between them.

The Labour critics of the government's foreign policy really fell into three categories. There were, first of all, the out-and-out pacifists who, like Lansbury before the war, preferred the entire abandonment of all military prepara-tion; secondly, there was a small band of crypto-Commun-ists, including a group of four or five Labour M.P.s and the officials of a number of unions controlled by the extreme Left, who could see nothing wrong in Russian foreign policy; and thirdly, there was a larger body of opinion, strong in the parliamentary party and focused in the 'Keep Left' group of M.P.s, who advocated the creation of a 'third force' of powers between Russia and America, and led by Britain. The 'Keep Left' group moved an amendment to the King's Speech in November 1946, but did not carry it to a vote. The policy, unfortunately, suffered from two defects: it took no account of the increasing tendency of political regimes outside the Communist sphere to swing in the direction of greater Conservatism; and it ignored the economic dependence of Britain and of other non-Communist powers upon the United States.

In the sphere of defence a revolt of seventy-two Labour M.P.s in April 1947 led to a rather undignified reversal of government policy, whereby the length of military service was cut from eighteen months to twelve. This appeared to be a victory for the Left: but an attempt to force the foreign policy issue at the Labour Party Conference of 1947 was easily defeated by Bevin. Speaking of the King's Speech amendment moved by the 'Keep Left' group, he described himself as having been 'stabbed in the back' by it, and added rather pointedly, 'I grew up in the trade union, you see, and I have never been used to this kind of thing'.[8] No card vote was called for after his speech, for it was obvious that he could rely upon the big battalions of the trade-union vote. After this, the 'Keep Left' revolt was virtually at an end. Only the pacifists and the crypto-Communists kept up their attacks, and continued to cause embarrassment to the government. The attitude of the pacifists was of course understandable, and had always been covered by the 'conscience clause' of Standing Orders; but the crypto-Communists were in a different case, and eventually they were all expelled from the party. They set up their own little party of 'Labour Independents' in the House. All of them were defeated in the 1950 election.

It remains to say a word about what will probably rank as the most important field of government policy — namely, the creation of the new states in Asia. Attlee, who had served on the Simon Commission for India, acted decisively by fixing a time-limit for the withdrawal of British troops from India, and he sent Lord Mountbatten as the last Viceroy to accomplish the transfer of power. In 1948, therefore, two new nations were created, India and Pakistan. Burma and Ceylon also achieved their independence. Yet of these four new states only Burma chose to sever its links with the Commonwealth. The situation in Palestine was less well handled, largely owing to the desire to keep on good terms with the Arab countries; and the withdrawal of British troops in 1948 was followed by a period of warfare between Jews and Arabs which ended in the establishment of the independent state of Israel.

(4)

The steady support of the labour movement outside Parliament for the work of the government was largely due to the trade-union leadership of the period. Bevin's position in the government was one of complete loyalty to Attlee, and his own record in the unions in turn guaranteed the government as a whole the fidelity of the major unions including his own Transport and General Workers, now ruled by his former assistant Arthur Deakin. The only real danger lay in the possibility that Communist infiltration of key posts in major unions might suddenly result in a change of policy. The danger became fully apparent after the alteration in the Communist 'line' in 1947, when in response to the initiative of the newly-founded 'Cominform' British Communists began to regard Attlee and Bevin as 'loyal supporters of the imperialists'.[9] Arthur Deakin and others then became seriously alarmed at the extent of Communist penetration of the unions; and accordingly the General Council of the T.U.C. issued a warning to the unions. In 1949 Deakin persuaded his own union to accept a rule preventing Communists from holding office; and this led to the dismissal of nine full-time officials at the end of the year. No such measure was possible in the Mineworkers or in the Engineers, which were both rather decentralised unions with strong existing pockets of Communist control. But in the Mineworkers the issue took the form of a stern disciplining of the Communist secretary, Arthur

Horner, by the President, Will Lawther, who had the executive on his side. In the General and Municipal Workers Union, the largest of the other unions, a rule banning Communists had been in operation ever since the 1920's. The Electrical Trades Union and the Fire Brigades Union, together with one or two smaller unions, were already wholly or largely under Communist control, but they did not constitute a very large voting element at party conferences. Under these circumstances, the unions gave their support to the government and accepted the policy of wage restraint — a policy unique in union history and inevitably dangerous for union officials to pursue for very long without risking the loss of their popularity with their members.

The collapse of the 'Keep Left' movement and the absorption of the party in the accomplishment of the legislative programme prevented any major open discords from damaging the party's chances at the impending general election. Cabinet differences there had been, particularly over iron and steel, but these had been largely hidden from the public. And, as we have seen, Attlee's position, with the support of Bevin, was unassailable. One remarkable achievement of the party in the period from 1945 to 1950 was that it had not lost a single seat at a by-election. At the beginning of 1950 the party prepared to stand upon its record, and indeed it had had little opportunity to work out a further detailed programme of nationalisation. The policy statement for the election, *Labour Believes in Britain*, which was again largely drawn up by Morrison, mentioned only sugar, cement, and water supply as industries suitable for public ownership within the period of the next Parliament.

Undoubtedly a swing against Labour was to be expected. The 'austerity' of the preceding years and the continuation of many shortages and many forms of rationing were naturally unpopular, and the government got the blame. Conservative party organisation was enormously better than in 1945, while the Labour party organisation had improved comparatively little. Furthermore, although the Representation of the People Act of 1948 abolished the university seats and the business vote, the advantage that the Labour Party thereby gained was more than offset by the redistribution of seats necessary to take account of population movement. The electoral system in the 1950's in fact had a slight 'bias' against the Labour Party, accounted for by the fact that the party's support in some exclusively working-class areas was so solid and uniform that it provided enormous Labour majorities, while the Conservative vote was less highly concentrated in a few constituencies and so more effective. It was calculated after the 1950 election, for instance, that with the Liberal vote at its existing level, the Conservative Party needed only 44·5 per cent of the total vote for its candidates in order to win a clear majority in the Commons, while Labour needed 46·5 per cent.[10] In the actual results, the Labour Party secured over 13¼ million votes — three-quarters of a million more than the Conservatives and 46·8 per cent of the total where it put up candidates. This gave it a very slight majority in the House : 315 seats, as against 298 for the Conservatives, 9 Liberals, and 2 Irish Nationalists. The closeness of the contest and the abolition of the university seats helped to eliminate the independents ; but the general verdict of the electorate could hardly be regarded as a decisive one. The working-class vote in favour of the Labour Party — never of course a complete one — had changed little, but there seemed to be a considerable defection of middle-class voters, for many seats in suburban London and the Home Counties reverted to Conservative allegiance. The overall swing from Labour to Conservative, if compared with 1945, was 3·3 per cent ; but in Wales it was only ·3 per cent, and in some parts of rural England it was less than 1 per cent.

According to Morrison, Attlee would have done better to delay the election from February, when it actually took place, to June : the Labour voters were always put off by bad weather, but would respond better in the warmer and lighter days of summer. Since the result was so close, there may have been something in this argument, but Attlee of course did not know beforehand what accidental misfortune might make things difficult for the party later in the year. At any rate, the result of the 1950 election closed a period of the party's history : it deprived it of its effective control of the legislature and began the decline in its parliamentary fortunes which has continued to the present day.

NOTES

1. Attlee to Laski, 1 May 1944, quoted Kingsley Martin, *Harold Laski* (1953), p. 161.
2. C. R. Attlee, *As It Happened* (1954), p. 132.
3. Attlee, *op. cit.* p. 156.
4. Herbert Morrison, *Autobiography* (1960), p. 245.
5. *Ibid.* p. 295.
6. Hansard, *Parliamentary Debates*, ser. 5, ccccxiii, 94.
7. Morrison, *op. cit.* p. 296.
8. *Labour Party Annual Report*, 1947, p. 179.
9. *World News and Views*, xxvii (1947), 463 f.
10. These figures and those that follow are taken from H. G. Nicholas, *British General Election of 1950* (1951).

FURTHER READING

For the years of the Coalition we are largely dependent upon volumes of memoirs, notably those by Attlee and Dalton which have already been mentioned, to which Emanuel Shinwell, *Conflict Without Malice* (1955), and Herbert Morrison, *Autobiography* (1960), should be added. There are some interesting letters published in Kingsley Martin, *Harold Laski*. On the period of the Labour Government, there is a rather sketchy outline of legislation and policy in Ernest Watkins, *The Cautious Revolution* (1951), and there is a sensible study of foreign policy in M. A. Fitzsimons, *Foreign Policy of the British Labour Government, 1945–1951* (Notre Dame, Ind., 1953).

There are also some valuable works of political analysis. Robert T. McKenzie's *British Political Parties* (1955) is useful for this period, and we also have the Nuffield election studies, starting with R. B. McCallum and A. Readman, *British General Election of 1945* (1947), and followed by H. G. Nicholas's volume for 1950. Two volumes dealing with the political links of the trade unions must also be mentioned : Martin Harrison, *Trade Unions and the Labour Party since 1945* (1960), and V. L. Allen, *Trade Unions and the Government* (1960).

ANEURIN BEVAN (1897–1960)

CHAPTER VII

Dissension and Decline

(*1950–60*)

(1)

THE main characteristics of the 1950's for the Labour Party were : public dissension among its leaders, and a decline of its popularity with the electorate. The two features were of course connected, though perhaps not as closely as some people may imagine, for, as we have seen, there had been plenty of open disagreements within the party in its long years of growth before the Second World War.

In the course of the decade the parliamentary leadership ceased to dominate the party as it had done in the 1940's. Attlee, of course, until his retirement in 1955, retained great prestige as the past and possible future Prime Minister ; but he was getting on in years (his seventieth birthday was in January 1953), and the great bulwark of his power in the party, Ernest Bevin, had been removed by death in 1951. On the other hand, the dissident Left, led by Aneurin Bevan, won much support among the active members of the constituency parties ; and as a result the National Executive, which was an important focus of power in the party when it was not in office, became a cockpit of conflict. Constitutionally, the Executive's functions were supposed to be in the sphere of administration rather than of policy, but the distinction had never been maintained in practice.

At first, it is true, the ultimate power in Conference seemed to remain in the hands of the major trade-union leaders, of whom the most important was Arthur Deakin, Bevin's successor as secretary of the Transport and General

Workers. It was largely Deakin and his colleagues Will Lawther of the Mineworkers and Tom Williamson of the General and Municipal Workers who in 1955 determined the succession to the party leadership. But Deakin died before his purpose was finally accomplished, and a few months later his own office as secretary of the Transport Workers fell to a left-wing militant, Frank Cousins — an event that immensely weakened the block of right-wing trade-union leaders in the party. Bevin and Deakin in their turn had been king-makers: Cousins so far has been no more than a *frondeur*. All the same, by 1960 the *fronde* had gone so far that the attempt of the party leader himself to take the initiative in shaping the party's destinies — most notably, by the revision of Clause Four of the constitution — resulted only in a face-saving compromise which suggested that positive leadership was temporarily impracticable.

(2)

The general election of February 1950 had given the Labour Party an overall Commons majority of only six, and this created a parliamentary situation that made government almost impossible. It was quite out of the question to attempt any contentious legislation, and the ordinary needs of administration could only be satisfied by great strain upon both ministers and M.P.s — for, however busy or ill they were, they were obliged to attend all important divisions in the House so as to save the government from premature defeat. Much to the fury of the Conservatives, the government allowed the nationalisation of iron and steel to take effect in February 1951. This could be done under the act which had passed on to the statute book in 1949.

Many of the government's difficulties, however, were caused by troubles within its own ranks. Several of its senior members were suffering from ill-health, and two of them, Bevin and Cripps, were forced to resign for that reason and shortly afterwards died. Cripps gave up the

Exchequer in October 1950, being succeeded by Hugh Gaitskell, now aged 44, who had proved his value as an efficient administrator in junior posts ; Bevin resigned the Foreign Office in February 1951 and was replaced by Herbert Morrison. The Prime Minister himself went into hospital at Easter, 1951, and almost immediately, without the steadying influence of the older leaders, dissensions began in the Cabinet. Faced by the heavy costs of the rearmament programme, which had been necessitated by the Korean War, Gaitskell in his budget decided to put charges upon the supply of dentures and spectacles under the National Health Service. This provoked the resignation in April 1951 of Bevan, who was now Minister of Labour, of Harold Wilson, who was President of the Board of Trade, and of John Freeman, Parliamentary Secretary to the Ministry of Supply.

Meanwhile, the government was still losing what popularity it had in the country. One cause of this was Morrison's handling of a dispute with Persia, which resulted in the expulsion of the staff of the Anglo-Iranian Oil Company by the Persian Government. Probably no stronger policy was practicable, especially in the absence of a mobile striking force ; but, in any case, Morrison was not experienced either in the conduct of foreign policy or in the art of explaining it to the country, as Bevin had been. Even more important, so far as the electorate was concerned, was the inflationary strain on the economy caused by the impact of the Korean War and the resulting rise in raw material and transport costs. The official index of prices, which in February 1950 stood at 113, rose rapidly in 1951 to a figure of 129 in October.

It was at this point that Attlee held a new election, probably with little hope of improving the Labour Party's position, but at least with the expectation that, one way or the other, stronger government would be assured. Naturally, the election, coming so soon after the very close result of 1950, was regarded as a renewed contest between the two major parties ; and so the Liberals and the candidates of smaller parties or the independents stood very little chance of election. Consequently the number of candidates was much smaller than in 1950. The main issues of the campaign were the cost of living and the danger of war: the Conservatives concentrated on the former, the Labour Party on the latter. According to Conservative speakers, Labour administration had led to a rapid devaluation of the pound; and Anthony Eden made a television broadcast on this theme, using a chart which was later strongly criticised on technical grounds by Labour. The Labour Party, for its part, maintained that the Conservative attitude on the Persian question showed that they were 'warmongers': the *Daily Mirror*, which was supporting Labour, came out with an election-day front page asking 'Whose Finger on the Trigger?'

In spite of its disadvantages the Labour Party secured the highest total poll that it or any other party has received up to the present day in a British general election: about fourteen million votes. The Conservatives received about a quarter of a million less, and yet won a majority of the seats. This was owing to the natural bias of the electoral system already mentioned. The new House therefore had 321 Conservative M.P.s, 295 Labour, 6 Liberals, and 3 Irish Independents. The Conservatives thus had an overall majority of 17 — a small figure, but two and a half times as large as that of Labour in 1950. The change of government was effected by a national swing of only 1·1 per cent of the voters — a swing, however, which was so remarkably uniform over the whole country as to cause rather too firm generalisations to be made about the homogeneity of the electorate. It must be remembered that regional and local variations in electoral behaviour always tend to be obscured if elections are held at such short intervals as that between February 1950 and October 1951.

On the whole, the Labour Party could regard these results with a reasonable degree of satisfaction. After all, it was no bad thing for a party exhausted by the tasks of administration to regroup itself in opposition, especially after an election which gave its opponents such a small majority and such a disappointing mandate. The danger was, however, that satisfaction would easily degenerate into complacency; and in the succeeding years the party paid all too little attention to the business of winning future elections. Instead, controversy within the ranks, already launched when Labour was in power, came to dominate its activities, absorbing much of the energies of the members; and party organisation, both at the centre and at the local level, suffered in consequence.

(3)

In March 1952 the conflict between the Bevanites, as the minority were called, and the parliamentary leadership came out into the open in a Commons debate on rearmament. Attlee and his colleagues had decided to move an amendment to the government motion on defence, but not to oppose the motion itself. Fifty-seven Labour M.P.s, however, did vote against the motion — a group which was later called 'the 57 varieties' because it contained a mixture of people with different motives — not only Bevan and his colleagues who had resigned from the government, but also the remnant of the old 'Keep Left' group including of course the pacifists. The revolt was less serious than it might seem, for Standing Orders, which had been suspended in 1946, had still not been reimposed, and so there was no formal breach of party discipline. But the result was the reimposition of Standing Orders, by decision of the parliamentary party, before the month was out. This meant that the parliamentary minority would be unable to express its views freely in the lobbies, and henceforward the battle would have to be fought outside Parliament. Anyone who voted contrary to the decision of the parliamentary party would risk expulsion and that, as was shown by the fate of independent candidates at recent general elections, would almost inevitably mean losing one's seat at the next contest.

Bevan's supporters in the parliamentary party were mostly nominees of the constituency parties, rather than of the trade unions; many of them were professional men, especially journalists. The leaders of the group, such as Michael Foot, Tom Driberg, and Richard Crossman, were active political columnists with plenty of opportunity to publicise their views and to try to win support. In *Tribune* they had their own political organ, and they could also make substantial use of the *New Statesman*. Neither of these weeklies was widely read by trade unionists, but both were much favoured by the constituency party rank and file. All the same, by far the greatest asset of the Bevanites was Bevan's own strong personality and his exceptional oratorical capacity.

The first major extra-parliamentary conflict came at the 1952 party conference. To the indignation of the leading union officials, no less than six of the seven constituency party seats on the Executive were won by the Bevanites, and both Morrison and Dalton were displaced. As it happened, Arthur Deakin was due to speak as fraternal delegate from the T.U.C., and he took the opportunity to demand the dissolution of the *Tribune* group, threatening the formation of counter-organisation if it continued. This apparently had its effect upon Attlee, for when the parliamentary party met later in the month, he demanded 'the immediate abandonment of all group organisation within the party other than those officially recognised'.[1] A resolution to this effect was carried by 188 votes to 51. Fifty-three M.P.s did not vote, owing to either absence or abstention. It was significant, however, that when in the following month the elections for the offices of the parliamentary party were held, Bevan obtained 82 votes against Morrison's 194 for the Deputy Leadership. Yet Bevan was the only one of his group to be elected to the Parliamentary Committee or 'shadow cabinet'.

By this time Attlee was almost seventy and was showing signs of tiredness. The question of succession had to be considered, and yet Morrison, who was the obvious claimant in many ways, had just suffered the ignominy of being thrown off the National Executive. The right-wing union leaders — Deakin, Lawther, and Williamson, who between them could guarantee about a third of the conference vote — offered Morrison their support for the Treasurership at the 1953 conference if he would stand against the ailing Greenwood, who had held the post since 1943. Morrison at first accepted, but when the conference was already in session he realised the strength of sentiment in favour of Greenwood, a respected incumbent in what was after all largely a sinecure. Morrison therefore withdrew, accepting a compromise whereby the Deputy Leader was given an *ex officio* place on the Executive. Morrison's chances of succeeding to the party leadership were not lost, but they were undoubtedly damaged by this manœuvre.

It was at this point that a fresh issue arose to divide the party and to give the Bevanites their greatest opportunity — the issue of German rearmament. The Churchill government had been persuaded by the Americans to accept the principle, but it was natural that the Opposition should have more difficulty in agreeing. After a discussion in the Parliamentary Labour Party, with Attlee and Morrison both urging acceptance, a favourable vote was carried by the small margin of 113 to 104. The issue came more fully into the open in April 1954, when Bevan resigned from the 'shadow cabinet', ostensibly because he was dissatisfied with the party's attitude on Far Eastern policy, but actually so as to take the lead in a campaign to reverse the decision over German rearmament at the forthcoming party conference. This action was likely to prejudice the party at the next election, which could not now be far in the future; and Harold Wilson, although nominally a Bevanite, consequently decided to accept the place in the 'shadow cabinet' which had been vacated by Bevan and for which, as it happened, he (Wilson) had been the runner-up in the parliamentary party's elections.

There were two main issues of conflict at the party's 1954 conference. One of them was the succession to the

Treasurership, now vacant owing to the death of Green-wood; the other was the issue of German rearmament. Morrison could not contest the Treasurership, now that he was on the Executive as Deputy Leader; and the trade-union leadership therefore put up Gaitskell as a rival to their enemy Bevan. Gaitskell had won the respect of the miners both because of his early work among them as a W.E.A. lecturer and more recently as Minister of Fuel. He now gained the support of Arthur Deakin and the other right-wing union leaders. As a result, he won, by over four million votes to Bevan's two million. It was not quite so easy, however, to put Bevan in the minority over German rearmament. This was a matter on which the rank and file of the party was deeply stirred, and it brought the Left a good deal of support which it could not normally expect. At the same time, this vote coming shortly before a general election would obviously be binding on the party, and thus it was a vital test for the leadership of Attlee and Morrison. In the upshot, the leadership was upheld by a majority of only a quarter of a million votes out of a total of six million. The decision was determined only by a last-minute switch on the part of the delegates of the Woodworkers and a few smaller unions which followed their lead.

Both decisions were galling for those who disliked the use of the unions' block vote, and not least so for the Bevan-ites and Bevan himself. He determined to continue his campaign to convert the party, and especially to try to win a foothold among the unions. At a meeting organised by *Tribune* before the conference was over he felt free to speak out about the decisions made, and it was on this occasion that he referred to Gaitskell — admittedly not very explicitly — as 'a desiccated calculating machine'. In point of fact, however, Gaitskell's capacity as an orator was steadily improving, and he proved able to hold his own on the platform of the party conference without any difficulty.

As the next election grew more and more imminent, so did the need for party unity increase. Yet early in 1955 Bevan gave yet another public parade of insubordination to the parliamentary leadership. It is true that the issue involved was one in which conscientious scruples were quite justified : the manufacture and use of the hydrogen bomb. The British Government's decision to make the bomb was announced in the Defence White Paper of 1955, and Bevan and his followers felt that this should not be accepted without some definite restrictions upon its use. The Bevanite group therefore expressed dissatisfaction with the official Opposition amendment to the motion approving the White Paper, and decided to abstain from voting. Altogether, a total of sixty-two Labour M.P.s abstained from the vote in this way : a gesture that was rather humiliating to the party leadership but which did not technically offend against Standing Orders, as abstention on grounds of conscience was permitted. But Bevan compounded his offence by interrupting Attlee's speech during the debate and putting a question to him. The 'shadow cabinet', under pressure from Morrison, therefore decided to withdraw the whip from Bevan, and this decision was rather reluctantly confirmed by the parliamentary party by a majority of 141 votes to 112.

It was clear that Morrison and the major trade-union leaders were anxious to have done with Bevan by expelling him from the party altogether. In particular, Arthur Deakin was active in lobbying members of the National Executive to secure this end. There were, however, many M.P.s and others who, while not agreeing with Bevan's views, felt that his expulsion would prove very damaging to the party. In the end, a compromise was proposed by Attlee on the National Executive and carried by 14 to 13. This enabled Bevan to retain his membership of the party after making an apology for his behaviour. An earlier initiative by Attlee might well have prevented the matter from being so fiercely debated : as always, he played a waiting game to the last moment — as Morrison put it, he 'doodled when he ought to have led'.[2] This, however, was the method by which Attlee had preserved his own position for so many years.

Only two weeks after this meeting of the National Executive, Churchill resigned from the Premiership, to be succeeded by Eden. Almost immediately the new Prime Minister decided on a general election, and this took place in May. The moment was a good one for the Conservatives, not only because of the controversy within the Labour Party, but because of the economic recovery of the time, which had enabled Butler as Chancellor of the Exchequer to make a number of tax cuts. Butler's budgets, not so very different from Gaitskell's when he had been Chancellor, had led to the coining of the word 'Butskellite' to describe the cautious and uncontroversial policy that both had pursued. Though the word was often used with opprobrium, the policy seemed on the whole to be popular, and it deprived the Labour Party of effective weapons of criticism. At the same time, the Labour Party suffered owing to its links with the unions, which were unpopular in the early summer of 1955 because of a number of strikes, each affecting a wide public. A newspaper strike, lasting almost a month, was followed during the election period by a dock strike and the threat of a rail strike : and both these latter disputes arose not out of direct conflict with employers but through inter-union rivalries.

The election was on the whole a quiet one. Both parties concentrated on the need for high-level meetings to secure peace, and the Labour Party failed to win any enthusiasm for its nationalisation proposals, which again comprehended steel and road haulage and added in 'sections of the chemical and machine-tool industries'. The electors were apathetic, meetings were generally small, partly, but only partly, owing to the use of television as a political medium ; and the Labour Party machine in particular was shown to be very rusty. Internal dissensions had weakened the party's efficiency, and it was significant that the number of full-time agents in the constituencies had dropped from 296 in 1951 to only 227. The Conservative Party, on the other hand, seemed as efficient as before. The result was that the Conservatives increased their parliamentary majority over all other parties from 17 in 1951 to 58. This was the first time for almost a century that a government had managed to increase its majority at a general election. The Labour Party's share of the poll dropped from 48·8 to 46·4 per cent, and was now less than the Conservative share by over 3 per cent. The swing from Labour to Conservative was about 1·8 per cent, but this time it was somewhat uneven in different parts of the country: it was substantially less in Scotland, perhaps owing to unemployment there, and substantially more in the Midlands where prosperity was greater. In East Anglia there was actually a slight swing to Labour: this was apparently due to the progress of the National Union of Agricultural Workers among the farm labourers there. The Conservatives now had a total of 344 M.P.s, while Labour had 277; the Liberals had 6 again and the Sinn Fein had 2.

Owing to the general apathy even the Conservative poll was down by some 400,000 compared with 1951; but the Labour poll had fallen by over 1½ million. Naturally enough, therefore, the Labour leaders drew the conclusion that their failure had been caused by the abstention of Labour voters, due to the party's internal differences and the weakness of its organisation. The National Executive immediately appointed a sub-committee under the chairmanship of Harold Wilson to enquire into the state of party organisation and report to the next party conference in October 1955. The committee found that many of the difficulties were beyond the control of the party: for instance, there had been a shortage of voluntary workers which had been due at least in part to full employment, overtime, and the employment of married women. But there were also serious faults in the work of full-time employees of the party and in the use of the party's funds. The report recommended the creation of a special sub-committee of the National Executive to supervise the work of organisation; special help in future for marginal constituencies; and a decentralisation of organisation to regional offices. An illustration of the poverty of the existing structure was given in the comment made in the report : 'We recommend that the necessary steps be taken to enable members of the Regional Staff to buy cars for use on organisation work'.³

(4)

All these matters should of course have been attended to in the years after the 1951 election, and one reason why they were not attended to, apart from the controversies within the party, was that the principal leaders were getting old and losing touch with the necessities of the new era. The recognition of this fact came soon after the 1955 defeat, and not only Attlee but also many of his colleagues gave up the positions of authority which they had so long held, in order to make way for younger men.

The fact that Attlee himself had clung to the leadership of the party for so long had encouraged others to stay with him in the 'shadow cabinet'. Attlee's motives have been subjected to some speculation : it may have been that he for his part wished to outlast Winston Churchill, who was more than eight years older than himself. Or it may have been that he recognised the difficulty of handing over to Morrison, when Morrison was both likely to widen the breach with the Bevanites and unable to secure the support of the constituency parties. But in any case, Attlee could hardly carry on much beyond the 1955 election.

When the new parliament assembled, Dalton, who had always been anxious to encourage the younger members of the party, decided that the time was ripe for his own resignation and for that of as many as possible of his elderly colleagues. He clearly wished to open the way to the leadership for his former protégé, Hugh Gaitskell. He therefore wrote to Attlee announcing his own retirement on grounds of age, and pointing out that no less than nine members of the 'shadow cabinet' were already over 65. He urged Attlee's retention of office 'in the interests of party unity', but was simultaneously putting pressure on his other colleagues to retire. In fact, four of them did so — among them being

Emanuel Shinwell and William Whiteley (the Chief Whip). Morrison remained, but he was now 67, and Dalton's remarks had built up an atmosphere of doubt about his capacity for high office in the future.

Meanwhile Gaitskell's ability as a parliamentary spokesman of the party became more and more obvious. It was this, together with the feeling that Morrison's best years were over, that swung the trade-union M.P.s to his support. Consequently, when Attlee at last resigned the leadership at the end of 1955, sentiment had crystallised in Gaitskell's favour and he was elected leader of the party by a substantial majority. The figures were : Gaitskell, 157 ; Bevan, 70 ; Morrison, 40. Morrison was taken aback by this result and refused to act as Deputy Leader ; the old middle-of-the-road stalwart James Griffiths was elected in his place. It was noteworthy, however, that Bevan, also standing for the Deputy Leadership, secured 111 votes against 141 for Griffiths : as Griffiths was the older man, this clearly suggested that if Bevan wanted to take the Deputy Leadership at some future date, he would be able to do so unless factional strife broke out once more.

It might be supposed that the election of Gaitskell, who had been considered more right-wing than Attlee, would be the signal for a fresh outburst of factional strife. But as was shown at the 1956 conference, the older right-wing block of trade-union votes had begun to disintegrate of its own accord. Bevan stood again for the Treasurership and this time won, securing the support of both the Mineworkers and the Railwaymen as well as of the constituency parties. The election of Frank Cousins, a left-wing militant, as secretary of the Transport and General Workers, the largest single voting unit in the conference, completed the picture of disarray on the right wing of the party.

Shortly afterwards there occurred the government's disastrous Suez operation, which solidified the Labour Party behind its leadership and revived, at least momentarily, the early prospect of a return to power. The government's policy was hotly debated both in Parliament and outside, and Gaitskell and Bevan in particular worked well together, both of them making effective fighting speeches. The National Council of Labour suddenly re-awoke to launch a popular campaign under the slogan 'Law not War'. Support for this came from people of all parties, especially intellectuals : and for a brief moment it was like the 1930's over again.

After the dust had begun to settle a little, in early 1957, it became clear that the Suez affair had both united the Labour Party and strengthened it in the constituencies. Gaitskell now felt able to give Bevan the post of 'shadow foreign secretary' which he had desired ; and the results of the by-elections showed the unpopularity of the government, which redounded to the advantage of Labour and Liberals alike. It was not so much that opposition to the Suez campaign had been general in the country — on the contrary, there was a strong feeling of popular jingoism which was evident even among regular Labour supporters — but rather that the increase in petrol prices and other temporary results of the failure of the campaign lowered the standing of the government.

It was the Labour Party's misfortune, however, that the collapse of Sir Anthony Eden placed a really formidable opponent, Harold Macmillan, in the office of Prime Minister. Combining to a remarkable degree the qualities of intelligence and toughness, Macmillan managed to rescue his party from the consequences of Suez, while simultaneously educating it to accept the lesson. Keeping domestic policy on a moderate 'Butskellite' line, he avoided antagonising the trade unions even at the cost of sacrificing his Chancellor of the Exchequer (Peter Thorneycroft) ; and he was able to let the country's increasing prosperity win approval for his government.

In the face of these adverse political circumstances, the Labour Party did its best to prepare for the next election. Unquestionably, it had learnt many of the lessons of its 1955 defeat. Internal dissension was muted, for Bevan supported the majority of the party on the issue of retention of the H-bomb, saying that Britain must not go 'naked into the conference chamber'.[4] The participation of both Bevan and Wilson in the 'shadow cabinet' deprived the rebellious minority of the party of its leadership, and the organisation that existed, known as the 'Victory for Socialism' group, had little influence. The party electoral organisation gradually improved: more agents were appointed and special attention was devoted to marginal constituencies. A new policy was carefully worked out: it concentrated on the need for economic expansion and growth with government encouragement, and maintained that this expansion would provide adequate funds for an expansion of social services. It advocated an elaborate scheme for improved pensions, and a more effective educational system involving the further encouragement of Comprehensive Schools. No industries were now scheduled for nationalisation except those that the Conservatives had denationalised — steel and road haulage; but the party reserved the right to make extensions of public ownership or control when necessary.

In the course of 1959 Macmillan gained popularity for his work in improving East-West relations and paving the way for a summit meeting. A considerable consumption boom also redounded to the credit of the government, and a long-term political advertising campaign both by the Conservative Party and by other bodies including the Iron and Steel Federation encouraged the formation of a favourable 'image' of the party in the country as a whole. When the dissolution of Parliament was announced in September 1959, towards the end of one of the finest summers in recent history, the result of the forthcoming election seemed to be already assured.

Yet the Labour Party could still stage a powerful and effective campaign. Gaitskell himself made a successful tour of the country, impressing many electors with his vigour and air of sincerity. The party's television broadcasts were better than those of the Conservatives, in an election in which television counted for more than ever before. Also, the headquarter press conferences run by the party secretary, Morgan Phillips, were unexpectedly successful and won much publicity in the newspapers. Halfway through the campaign it seemed as if Labour was drawing equal with the Conservatives. At this stage, however, Labour spokesmen published various pledges not to increase taxation, and these could be construed as bribes to the electorate : it was easy for their opponents to take advantage of this. The campaign ended with opinion apparently swinging back in the Conservative favour.

The results gave the Conservative Party a considerably increased majority — a unique success for a party that had been in office already for eight years. The new House contained 365 Conservatives, 258 Labour, and 6 Liberal members, together with one Independent. The Labour share of the poll had dropped from 46·4 to 43·8 per cent; and the Liberals had more than doubled their share, partly through running more candidates and partly by increasing their vote in many of the contests. Only in Scotland and in Lancashire and Cheshire, where there was some industrial unemployment, did the Labour Party improve its position compared with 1955.

(5)

To lose three consecutive elections, by an increasing margin on each occasion — this was the fate of the Labour Party in the 1950's. It was natural that the failure of 1959 should be followed by a much more searching phase of self-examination than the party had ever undertaken before. Was the Labour Party, with its 'class' basis and its close ties with the unions, obsolete in the new Britain? Was the Liberal revival indicative of a need for a new alignment on the Left? Gaitskell himself, speaking at the brief conference of the party held a few weeks after the election, narrowed the issue to the demand for a revision of the party's objects, as laid down in the constitution. He urged the abandonment of the existing Clause Four, with its demand for 'the common ownership of the means of pro-

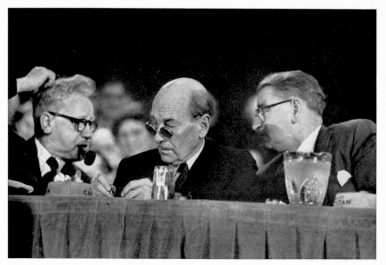

ATTLEE WITH HERBERT MORRISON (left) AND MORGAN PHILLIPS

HUGH GAITSKELL (b. 1906)

duction, distribution, and exchange'. After a sharp controversy within the party, however, he was forced to accept a compromise whereby the National Executive was committed to recommending the retention of the existing clause and the addition of a new statement of principles.

But soon the disagreements over the revision of the constitution were swallowed up in a larger controversy over the party's defence policy. The Campaign for Nuclear Disarmament, which advocated the unilateral renunciation of atomic weapons, had been winning many recruits within the party, particularly among the younger generation; and when Gaitskell in consultation with both party and T.U.C. leaders drew up a new statement of defence policy in the summer of 1960, he found himself faced by strong opposition from the Left wing — not only the Nuclear Disarmers but also a variety of opponents ranging from out-and-out pacifists and Communist sympathisers to a more opportunistic group who — after Gaitskell's opposition to Clause Four — wished primarily to change the party leadership. What gave this new alliance particular strength was its success in marshalling the union block vote, for in addition to the usual Left minority among the unions, Frank Cousins swung the Transport Workers against the current defence policy. The struggle reached a climax at the T.U.C. meeting in September and at the Labour Party Conference in October. At the T.U.C. the official defence policy statement was approved, but so was a conflicting resolution from the Transport Workers — a Gilbertian situation resulting from the compromise efforts of the Engineers' leader, W. J. Carron. At the ensuing Labour Party Conference, held at Scarborough, Gaitskell, deprived of the support both of Bevan (who had recently died) and of Morgan Phillips (who was seriously ill), fought fiercely for the defence policy statement. After a dramatic debate in which he and his ablest colleagues evidently won most of the uncommitted votes of the divisional party delegates, the statement was narrowly defeated and a resolution favouring unilateral disarmament was even more narrowly carried by a union block vote which had been determined before the debate.

A situation entirely unprecedented in the party's history had now arisen. Not only had the policy of the parliamentary leader been defeated by conference on a major issue; the vote had also caused a rift between the conference majority and the majority of the parliamentary party, who still remained committed to nuclear defence. Supported as he was by the ablest remaining parliamentary spokesmen and by the bulk of the constituency parties, Gaitskell announced that he would 'fight and fight and fight again' to secure the reversal of the decision. It remained to be seen whether he could for long remain as leader of the parliamentary party when defying a major conference decision, however narrowly carried : certainly such a situation offended against the radical traditions of the party and threatened many difficulties and embarrassments for the future. At the opening of the new parliamentary session in November he was re-elected by 166 votes as against 81 for Harold Wilson, who advocated a policy of compromise with the conference majority. Gaitskell's supporter George Brown was elected Deputy Leader in succession to Bevan. Meanwhile, partisans of both sides indulged in mutual recriminations.

Thus the last months of 1960 saw the Labour Party in a weaker state than at any time for a generation : its leadership in dispute, its policy equally indeterminate on major issues, its constitution under heavy strain, and its prestige humbled. The Liberal Party challenge, although not yet able to make any impact on the parliamentary situation, was looming on the horizon. A new phase of the Labour Party's history was about to begin : but none could tell whether it led still more steeply downwards into electoral disaster, or whether events would permit a rallying of the various factions in time for future challenges.

Dissension and Decline (1950–60)

NOTES

1. *The Times*, 24 Oct. 1952.
2. Morrison, *Autobiography*, p. 295.
3. *Labour Party Annual Report*, 1955, p. 69.
4. *Labour Party Annual Report*, 1957, p. 181.

FURTHER READING

For a journalistic but well-informed account of the controversies within the Labour ranks, see Leslie Hunter, *Road to Brighton Pier* (1959). For left-wing attitudes to questions of foreign policy in the first post-war decade, see Leon D. Epstein, *Britain: Uneasy Ally* (Chicago, 1954).

Different views of the party's power-structure and the role of the party conference are put by Robert T. McKenzie in his *British Political Parties* and by Saul Rose, 'Policy Discussion in Opposition', *Political Studies*, iv (1956), pp. 126-38. See also Robert T. McKenzie, 'Policy Decisions in Opposition: A Rejoinder', *Political Studies*, v (1957), pp. 176-82. Although Mr. McKenzie's book is of lasting importance, it completely fails to comprehend the role of the trade-union leadership within the party.

Martin Harrison's *Trade Unions and the Labour Party since 1945* is also important for this period, as are the Nuffield election studies for 1951, 1955, and 1959, all of them partially or wholly prepared by David Butler.

CHAPTER VIII

Conclusion: *The Past and the Future*

ALTHOUGH political parties possess a certain organic
character, it is not easy to analyse their structure in precise
biological terms, or to predict their processes of adaptation
or decay. The Labour Party, although unique in many
ways, is no exception in this respect. Many of the generalisations that may be attempted to describe its effective
working and development soon come to need qualification;
and forecasts of its future behaviour must be tentative in
character.

The party was founded to represent a class interest
in Parliament, and its formal tie both with the trade unions
and with the Socialists reflects this fact. And yet right from
the start it began to pick up many of the traditional features
of Liberalism, usually regarded as the ethos of the middle
class: the support of religious Nonconformity, the advocacy
of Free Trade, the creed of internationalism of the Bright
and Cobden variety. During and after the First World
War the Liberal Party began to disintegrate, and the
Liberal intellectuals began to move over to the Labour
Party, thus perpetuating the tendency of the party to find
its support to some extent across, rather than within, the
boundaries of class.

Originally, the control of the party depended a good
deal upon the efforts of the most enthusiastic supporters of
the 'Labour Alliance' — the I.L.P. leaders, and particularly Ramsay MacDonald, who was the party secretary.
Arthur Henderson, who succeeded MacDonald as secretary,
also had his period of almost unchallenged authority. But
the annual conference was always important, and its public
debates, unlike those of the National Liberal Federation or

the National Union of Conservative Associations, resulted in decisions that normally became binding upon the party as a whole. In time, however, the parliamentary party asserted more and more discretion for itself; and the smooth running of the whole organisation, and a reasonable degree of harmony between leadership and Conference, came to depend upon effective liaison between the parliamentary leaders and those trade-union officials who wielded the largest block votes at Conference.

This liaison of parliamentary and trade-union leaders has not been easy to maintain, especially since the parliamentary party grew in size and came within reach of power; and it has been hindered by the fact that the major trade-union leaders since the 1920's have been too preoccupied with their union duties and with membership of the T.U.C. General Council to maintain constant contact with parliamentary affairs. Thus it was that the conflict of Ramsay MacDonald and the General Council of the T.U.C. in 1931 was preceded by several years in which liaison had been slight and unfriendly. It was in an effort to overcome this difficulty that the National Council of Labour was set up on a new basis in 1932: but the situation of that time, with a shrunken and ineffective parliamentary leadership, meant that Bevin and Citrine for a few years controlled the parliamentary party by a curious 'indirect rule'. Later on, the mild and pliant Attlee — a master of the *coup de repos* — won Bevin's confidence, and a period of good relations ensued that lasted until 1950. Only in recent years has the liaison again proved unsatisfactory, partly as a result of Gaitskell's attempt to force the pace of constitutional reform within the party, and partly owing to the accident that the mantle of Bevin has fallen upon a militant of the Left in Frank Cousins. Even in a great organisation like the Labour Party, where so much constitutional emphasis is placed upon mass voting, the power of individual personality in practice still counts for a great deal.

Since the 1959 general election, which was the party's third defeat in succession, there have been many gloomy prophecies about the future prospects of Labour, and these views have gained added justification as a result of the present internal convulsions of the party. And yet we must bear in mind to what extent the outcome of a general election depends upon circumstances that have little to do with the real merits of the political parties. Had the Conservative Government been forced to go to the polls in 1957 or even in 1958, it is probable that there would now be a Labour Government, and that the party's leader, as Prime Minister, would be steadily consolidating his pre-eminence over his colleagues. While the Labour Party remains at least the second largest party in the Commons, it remains the alternative government of the country, and is the direct beneficiary of any discontent that the policies of the existing government may incur, whether deservedly or not. It would therefore be a rash prediction that the future leaders of the Labour Party, whoever they may be, will never again find themselves in popular favour, and able to take their places once more upon the Treasury Bench.

APPENDIX A

PARTY MEMBERSHIP

Date	Individual Membership	T.U. Membership	Co-operative Societies Membership*	Socialist Societies etc. Membership	Total
1900–1	Nil	353,070	Nil	22,861	375,931
1901–2	Nil	455,450	Nil	13,861	469,311
1902–3	Nil	847,315	Nil	13,835	861,150
1903–4	Nil	956,025	Nil	13,775	969,800
1904–5	Nil	855,270	Nil	14,730	900,000
1905–6	Nil	904,496	Nil	16,784	921,280
1906–7	Nil	975,182	2,271	20,885	998,338
1907	Nil	1,049,673	472	22,267	1,072,413†
1908	Nil	1,127,035	565	27,465	1,158,565
1909	Nil	1,450,648	678	30,982	1,486,308
1910	Nil	1,394,403	760	31,377	1,430,539
1911	Nil	1,501,783	911	31,404	1,539,092
1912	Nil	1,858,178	1,073	31,237	1,895,498
1913	Nil	Not compiled‡	1,328	33,304	Not compiled‡
1914	Nil	1,572,391	1,526	33,230	1,612,147
1915	Nil	2,053,735	1,792	32,828	2,093,365
1916	Nil	2,170,782	1,792	42,190	2,219,764
1917	Nil	2,415,383	2,608	47,140	2,465,131
1918	Not compiled	2,960,409	Nil	52,720	3,013,129
1919	„	3,464,020	Nil	47,270	3,511,290
1920	„	4,317,537	Nil	42,270	4,359,807
1921	„	3,973,558	Nil	36,803	4,010,361
1922	„	3,279,276	Nil	31,760	3,311,036
1923	„	3,120,149	Nil	35,762	3,155,911
1924	„	3,158,002	Nil	36,397	3,194,399
1925	„	3,337,635	Nil	36,235	3,373,870
1926	„	3,352,347	Nil	35,939	3,388,286
1927	„	3,238,939	20,000	34,676	3,293,615
1928	214,970	2,025,139	20,000	32,060	2,292,169
1929	227,897	2,044,279	32,000	26,669	2,330,845
1930	277,211	2,011,484	32,000	26,213	2,346,908
1931	297,003	2,024,216	32,000	4,847	2,358,066

Appendix A: Party Membership—contd.

Date	Individual Membership	T.U. Membership	Co-operative Societies Membership*	Socialist Societies etc. Membership	Total
1932	371,607	1,960,269	32,040	7,871	2,371,787
1933	366,013	1,899,007	32,040	7,970	2,305,030
1934	381,259	1,857,524	22,040	7,667	2,278,490
1935	419,311	1,912,924	36,000	9,280	2,377,515
1936	430,694	1,968,538	36,000	9,125	2,444,357
1937	447,150	2,037,071	37,333	6,118	2,527,672
1938	428,826	2,158,076	37,333	6,054	2,630,286
1939	408,844	2,214,070	37,333	2,820	2,663,067
1940	404,124	2,226,575	37,333	3,131	2,571,163
1941	226,622	2,230,728	25,200	2,908	2,485,458
1942	218,783	2,206,209	25,200	3,740	2,453,932
1943	235,501	2,237,307	25,200	5,232	2,503,240
1944	265,763	2,375,381	25,200	6,501	2,672,845
1945	487,047	2,510,369	33,600	7,681	3,038,697
1946	645,345	2,635,346	33,600	8,067	3,322,358
1947	608,487	4,386,074	36,960	8,778	5,040,299
1948	629,025	4,751,030	33,600	8,782	5,422,437
1949	729,624	4,946,207	33,600	7,516	5,716,947
1950	908,161	4,971,911	30,800	9,300	5,920,172
1951	876,275	4,937,427	28,000	7,300	5,849,002
1952	1,014,524	5,071,935	14,000	7,200	6,107,659
1953	1,004,685	5,056,912	28,000	7,425	6,096,022
1954	933,657	5,529,760	28,000	7,610	6,498,027
1955	843,356	5,605,988	28,000	7,650	6,483,994
1956	845,129	5,658,249	28,000	6,850	6,537,228
1957	912,987	5,644,012	20,000	5,550	6,582,549
1958	888,955	5,627,690	20,000	5,541	6,542,186
1959	847,526	5,564,010	20,000	5,450	6,436,986

* This does not include the membership of the Co-operative Party (founded in 1917).

† The totals between 1907 and 1917 in this column also include membership of the Women's Labour League.

‡ Trade-union membership figures could not be compiled for 1913 owing to the operation of the Osborne Judgment.

APPENDIX B

GENERAL ELECTION RESULTS

Date	Seats Contested	Members Returned	Total Votes Polled
1900	15	2	62,698
1906	50	29	323,195
1910 (Jan.)	78	40	505,690
1910 (Dec.)	56	42	370,802
1918	361	57	2,244,945
1922	414	142	4,236,733
1923	427	191	4,348,379
1924	514	151	5,487,620
1929	569	287	8,364,883
1931	491	46	6,362,561
1935	539	154	8,325,260
1945	604	393	11,992,292
1950	617	315	13,295,736
1951	617	295	13,948,385
1955	620	277	12,405,246
1959	621	258	12,216,166

APPENDIX C

CHAIRMEN OF THE PARLIAMENTARY PARTY

Note — In 1922 the designation was changed from 'Chairman' to 'Chairman and Leader'

1906–8	J. Keir Hardie
1908–10	Arthur Henderson
1910–11	George Barnes
1911–14	J. Ramsay MacDonald
1914–17	Arthur Henderson
1917–21	W. Adamson
1921–22	J. R. Clynes
1922–31	J. Ramsay MacDonald
1931–32	Arthur Henderson
1932–35	George Lansbury
1935–55	C. R. Attlee
1955–	Hugh Gaitskell

APPENDIX D

PARTY SECRETARIES

1900–12	J. Ramsay MacDonald
1912–34	Arthur Henderson
1935–44	J. S. Middleton
1944–	Morgan Phillips

INDEX

Adamson, W., 46, 49
Addison, Lord, 96
Alexander, A. V., 89, 96
Angell, Norman, 37
Anglo-Iranian Oil Co., 107
Asquith, H. H., 29, 38, 39
Attlee, Clement, 50, 65, 75, 79; party
  leader, 80, 81, 84, 85, 86, 88;
  Coalition minister, 89, 91 f., 93 f.;
  Prime Minister, 95-7, 98, 101, 102,
  103 f., 107, 125; continues as
  leader, 105, 110, 113, 116, 117

Baldwin, Stanley, 55, 80
Balfour, Arthur, 16
Bank of England, 96
Barnard Castle by-election (1903), 14
Barnes, George, 9, 20, 32, 39, 41,
  45 f.
Bell, Richard, 10, 11, 14
Belloc, Hilaire, 26
Bevan, Aneurin, 84, 97, 98 f., 105, 107,
  109-13, 117-19, 121, 122
Bevanites, 109-13
Beveridge Report (1942), 92, 96, 98
Bevin, Ernest: Transport Workers'
  leader, 47, 54; role in 1931, 67-9;
  controls party, 71 f., 77, 79, 80, 82,
  83, 106, 125; Coalition minister,
  89, 90, 92; Foreign Secretary, 95,
  98, 99, 106 f.; relations with
  Attlee, 81, 89, 96, 101, 102, 105,
  125
'Black and Tans', 49
Blatchford, Robert, 25
Boot and Shoe Workers, National
  Union of, 9
Braithwaite, W. J., 22
Bright, John, 124
British Broadcasting Corporation
  (B.B.C.), 91
British Electricity Authority, 97
British Road Services, 97
British Socialist Party (B.S.P.), 25, 30,
  31, 32, 40, 49
British Transport Commission, 96 f.
Brown, George, 122
Butler, R. A., 114

Campbell, J. R., 58 f.
Campbell-Bannerman, Sir H., 16
Carron, W. J., 121
Catering Wages Act (1943), 92
Chamberlain, Joseph, 13, 45
Chamberlain, Neville, 73, 84, 85, 86
Chelmsford, Lord, 56
Chesterton, G. K., 26
'Chinese Labour', 14, 15
Churchill, Winston, 60, 84, 85, 96,
  111, 114, 116; Coalition Premier,
  86, 88, 90, 91, 93; criticises Labour
  constitution, 93 f., 95
Clarion, 25
Clarion Fellowship, 25
Clause Four, 43 f., 106, 120, 121
Clitheroe by-election (1902), 12
Clynes, J. R., 45 f., 49, 52 f., 56,
  81
Coal Industry Royal Commission
  (1925–6), 60
Coit, Stanton, 16
Cole, G. D. H., 26, 69
Colne Valley by-election (1907),
  22
Communist Information Bureau
  (Cominform), 101
Communist International (Comin-
  tern), 62, 82, 84
Communist Party, 49 f., 53 f., 62, 74,
  79, 81, 82, 84, 101 f., 121
Comprehensive Schools, 119
Conscription, 38 f., 85 f., 100
Conspiracy and Protection of Property
  Act (1875), 6
Contracting In or Out. *See* Political
  Levy
Co-operative Party, 47, 64
Co-operative Union, 46 f., 89
Cotton Weavers, Northern Counties
  Amalgamated, 12, 20
Council of Action, 47
Cousins, Frank, 106, 117, 121, 125
Credit Anstalt, 66
Cripps, Sir Stafford, 75, 76, 79, 83 f.,
  89, 90, 91, 98, 106 f.
Crooks, Will, 14
Crossman, Richard, 110

Index

Johnston, Thomas, 64, 90, 92
Jolly George, 47
Jowett, Fred, 56, 64
Jowitt, Sir William, 89

'Keep Left' group, 99 f., 102, 109
Keynes, J. M., 62, 69
Korean War, 107

Labour, National Council of. *See* National Joint Council
Labour and the Nation (1928), 63, 65
Labour and the New Social Order (1918), 44, 63
Labour Believes in Britain (1950), 102
Labour Electoral Committee, 8
Labour Government, First (1924), 56-9; Second (1929-31), 64-7; Third (1945-51), 88, 95-103, 106-8
Labour Party (*originally* Labour Representation Committee), constitution, 8 f., 12 f., 43-5, *and see* Clause Four; local or divisional parties of, 13, 30, 31, 43, 44, 46, 53 f., 55, 63, 83, 105, 110; National Executive, composition of, 9 f., 39 f., 43, 44, 83, 105; parliamentary party, Standing Orders of, 21, 95, 100, 109, 113; exclusion of Communists from, 49 f., 51 f., 83 f.
Labour Representation League, 7
Lansbury, George, 22, 26, 27, 53; minister, 64, 67 f.; party leader, 75, 77, 78, 79 f., 99
Laski, Harold, 83, 84, 93
Lawther, Will, 101, 106, 111
League of Nations, 42, 58, 78
League of Nations Union, 80
Lees Smith, H. B., 90
Left Book Club, 83
Lend-Lease, American, 98
Let Us Face the Future (1945), 94
Let Us Reform the Labour Party (1910), 24 f.
'Lib-Lab' M.P.s, 7, 12, 18
Location of Industry Act (1945), 92
Locomotive Engineers, Associated Society of, 26
London County Council, 31, 78
London Labour Party, 31, 78
London Trades Council, 31
Lyons v. Wilkins (1898), 6, 11

MacDonald, J. Ramsay, party secretary, 8, 13, 14, 15, 19, 20, 24, 124; parliamentary chairman, 22, 27,

31 f., 33, 35 f., 36 f.; opposes First World War, 35-7, 40, 42, 46; Leader of Opposition, 52 f., 60, 62 f.; Prime Minister, 58-60, 67 f., 71-4, 80; memory of, in party, 78, 88 f., 94
MacDonald, Malcolm, 68
MacDonald-Gladstone electoral agreement (1903), 13, 14, 19, 33
Macmillan, Harold, 118, 119
Mann, Tom, 25 f.
'Marshall Plan', 99
Maxton, James, 55, 62
'Memorandum on War Aims' (1917), 42
Middleton, J. S., 68, 78
Miners Federation, 42, 45, 48, 75
Mineworkers, National Union of, 101, 106, 117
Ministers of the Crown Act (1937), 90
Morel, E. D., 37
Morris, William, 3
Morrison, Herbert, 78, 79, 80, 81, 82, 85; Coalition minister, 89, 90, 91, 94; Lord President, 94, 95 f., 97, 102, 103; Foreign Minister, 107; fails to win leadership, 110 f., 112, 113, 116, 117
Mosley, Sir Oswald, 64, 65, 66, 74
Mountbatten, Lord, 100 f.
Munich Agreement (1938), 84, 94
Mussolini, Benito, 79

National Coal Board, 96
National Council of Labour. *See* National Joint Council
National Free Labour Association, 5
National Insurance Act (1911), 27; (1946), 98
National Joint Council (*later* National Council of Labour), 49, 59; reorganised to control party, 77, 78, 79, 82, 88, 125; role of, in foreign policy, 79, 80, 84, 85, 118; loses power, 89
National Labour group, 73, 74, 80
National Left Wing Movement, 54, 62
National Liberal Federation, 13, 124
National Union of Conservative Associations, 125
New Fabian Research Bureau, 76
New Party, 66, 74
New Statesman, 81, 110
Nonconformity, 13, 16, 30, 124

Index

THE END

PRINTED BY R. & R. CLARK, LTD., EDINBURGH